Methods, Ethics and Models

Social Science Lexicons

Key Topics of Study
Key Thinkers, Past and Present
Political Science and Political Theory
Methods, Ethics and Models
Social Problems and Mental Health

Methods, Ethics and Models

Edited by Jessica Kuper

ROUTLEDGE & KEGAN PAUL
LONDON AND NEW YORK

First published in 1987 by
Routledge & Kegan Paul Limited
11 New Fetter Lane, London EC4P 4EE

Published in the USA by
Routledge & Kegan Paul Inc.
in association with Methuen Inc.
29 West 35th Street, New York, NY 10001

Set in Linotron Baskerville
by Input Typesetting Ltd., London SW19 8DR
and printed in Great Britain
by Cox & Wyman Ltd
Reading, Berks

Library of Congress Cataloging in Publication Data

Social science encyclopedia. Selections.
  Methods, ethics, and models.

  (Social science lexicons)
  Includes bibliographies and index.
  1. Social sciences—Dictionaries. I. Kuper,
Jessica. II. Title. III. Series.
H41.S6325 1987b   300'.1   87-4277

British Library CIP Data also available
ISBN 0-7102-1172-4

Contents

Methods, Ethics and Models: the entries

Contributor List

General Editor: Jessica Kuper

Alexander, Jeff   Dept of Sociology, University of California, Los Angeles

Barrell, Ray   Dept of Economics, University of Southampton

Bartley, W W III   Dept of Philosophy, California State University at Hayward and The Hoover Institution, Stanford

Bloor, David   Science Studies Unit, University of Edinburgh

Boissevain, Jeremy   Dept of Anthropology, University of Amsterdam

Bracher, Michael   Australian National University, Canberra

Bulmer, Martin   Dept of Social Administration, The London School of Economics and Political Science

Cohen, Percy S   Dept of Sociology, The London School of Economics and Political Science

Colman, Andrew   Dept of Psychology, University of Leicester

Cowan, Charles D   Bureau of the Census, Washington DC

Doreian, Patrick   Dept of Sociology, University of Pittsburgh

Douglas, Susan P   Graduate School of Business Administration, New York University

Draguns, Juris G   Dept of Psychology, Pennsylvania State University

Fienberg, Stephen E   Dept of Statistics, Carnegie-Mellon University, Pittsburgh

Geer, John van de   Dept of Psychology, University of Leiden

Gilgen, Albert R	Dept of Psychology, University of Northern Iowa, Cedar Falls
Glickman, Maurice	Dept of Sociology, University of Botswana
Goyder, John	Dept of Sociology, University of Waterloo, Ontario
Hage, Per	Dept of Anthropology, University of Utah
Hanson, F Allan	Dept of Anthropology, University of Kansas
Harary, Frank	Institute for Social Research, University of Michigan, Ann Arbor
Jarvie, I C	Dept of Philosophy, York University, Downsview, Ontario
Kassiola, Joel	Dept of Political Science, Brooklyn College, City University of New York
Keil, Charles	Dept of American Studies, State University of New York at Buffalo
Kellner, Douglas	Dept of Philosophy, University of Texas at Austin
Kiiveri, Harry	Dept of Mathematics and Statistics, CSIRO Institute of Physical Sciences, Wembley, Western Australia
Klir, George J	Dept of Systems Science, State University of New York at Binghampton
Krathwohl, David R	School of Education, Syracuse University, Syracuse, NY
Runyan, William McKinley	School of Social Welfare, University of California, Berkeley
Santow, Gigi	Dept of Demography, Research School of Social Sciences, The Australian National University
Smith, James E	Cambridge Group for the History of Population and Social Structure, University of Cambridge

Stone, Mervyn — Dept of Statistical Sciences, University College, London

Thompson, John B — Jesus College, University of Cambridge

Tjon Sie Fat, Franklin — Dept of Cultural Anthropology, University of Leiden

Van der Ven, A H G S — Dept of Psychology, Catholic University of Nijmegen, The Netherlands

Weale, Martin — Dept of Applied Economics, University of Cambridge

Philosophy of the Social Sciences

Philosophy of the social sciences is, in the bureaucratic jargon of academe, the study of the aims and methods of the social sciences (sociology, anthropology, political science, psychology, sometimes economics; borderline cases are history, geography, demography and linguistics); it constitutes a subspecialty within philosophy of science – the study of the aims and methods of science in general. Standard anthologies organize their material around such questions as: are natural things fundamentally different from social things; must then the sciences of social things use different methods from the sciences of natural things; are then sciences of the social at all possible; alternatively, are social things mere aggregates; do social things mix facts and values; are values a social product? From this list it is apparent that the subject is engaged with traditional philosophical concerns: ontological, epistemological and normative.

Rarely is there a perfect fit between a subject as defined by academic bureaucracy and what its practitioners actually do. And when place is found for transcendental arguments to the effect that the 'subject' is an impossibility, this cannot but affect an encyclopaedia article. All alternative frameworks have their limitations. An Aristotelian matrix approach, dividing the subject up into orderly categories and concepts, conceals unruly and disorderly elements. The historical approach, treating it as a story with a beginning, a middle and, possibly, an end, risks identifying the subject with present preoccupations. The kinship approach, tracing all present elements to a common ancestor, risks merging and simplifying descent. The map-making approach, trying to give an overall picture, has to ignore continental drift. My choice is a metaphysical sketch map, supplemented by a little history. The result will be a trifle untidy, but the reader should be aware this is because the terrain itself is mountainous, dotted with mists, and we are forced to map from sea-level, without radar.

Nature and Convention

The phrase 'philosophy of the social sciences' itself suggests that there is scientific study of the social (denied by phenomenologists and some followers of Wittgenstein, see below), and that the aims and methods of such study may differ from those of science in general (denied by the logical positivists and others, see below). The very distinction between the natural and the social, between nature and convention, is deeply rooted in our thinking. It was not always so, but it is the notion of impersonal nature that is recent. Once, mankind took itself as the measure of all things and explained nature anthropomorphically; the result of the scientific revolution (in ancient Greece and post-Renaissance Western Europe – we concentrate on the latter) was to overthrow anthropomorphism, to depersonalize nature and explain it by postulating orderly and law-like processes unfolding mechanically (Dijksterhuis, 1961). Such was the flush of seventeenth- and eighteenth-century enthusiasm for the new science that even man himself was to be treated as part of nature, a machine, his works by 'social physics', his aims and desires as motive forces – or motives for short – and his actions as movements, including social movements and social revolutions akin to the revolving of the heavens.

Such euphoria came to grief over problems like how to maximize the creation of wealth; how to realize moral and political aims in social institutions; how to prevent suicide; which seemed to demand, if not anthropomorphism, then, at least, laws of human convention. If nature is taken to be those aspects of things that are more or less given, the laws and motive forces governing which we cannot alter, then convention covers all forms of orderliness that we attribute to human efforts, orderliness that is not constant from place to place and time to time, and which is humanly alterable. This division of our environment into unchanging and changing parts affects our efforts to explain it. It makes it our first task when facing a problem to decide whether it belongs to nature or to convention – usually a far from uncontroversial allocation.

Controversy over what is natural and what is conventional is heightened by the presence of established sciences of nature. A metaphysical issue is given a methodological twist. This comes about as follows: the rise and success of natural science is, it is widely held, to be explained as the application of a particular method, the empirical method. Thus, if a problem is identified as natural, the methods of the natural sciences are appropriate; but having been so successful with nature perhaps they are appropriate for problems of convention also. To the ancient Greeks this might have seemed absurd. But as European society under industrialization changed from *Gemeinschaft* to *Gesellschaft*, more systematic thought had to be given to altering current conventions and making them work better. As such social thought grew in cognitive power and practical importance, debates about the boundary between nature and convention, and hence the appropriate methods with which to approach convention, took on a life of their own. Some philosophers of social science, greatly exercised over questions of method, are unaware that they debate a disguised metaphysical issue. One example of this is those who push the empirical method because they hold that nature is real and observable, whereas conventions are abstract unobservables (Kaufman, 1944). A relic of this thinking is the individualism/holism dispute over what is more and what is less real among conventions. One party, the individualists, holds that only individual human beings are real and larger-scale social entities are aggregates which can be, for explanatory purposes, reduced to theories about individuals. The other party, the holists, questions the reality of individuals when they can be explained as creatures of society. Although there is some purely philosophical debate of such issues, under the influence of positivism they are usually joined in methodological form: which is more empirically observable – the individual or the whole? A convincing case can be made for either side.

Awkwardly cutting across all attempts to map this field are

Marxist variants of each set of issues. Marx could be said to hold that there was only nature, not convention, and that his 'dialectical materialism' should be seen as part of natural science. The cross-cutting occurs because Marxists will not permit him to be treated as just one of a succession of social scientists; hence they dispute the interpretation of Marx's writings, while others advance positions they claim are in the spirit of his work, if not within the letter. As a result almost every issue in the philosophy of the social sciences is duplicated within Marxism, but in a manner that exaggerates the importance of Marx. Mainstream philosophers of social science often mention Marx, but he is a pivotal figure only for Marxists.

Positivism and its Legacy

Empiricist methodology always had its a priorist opponents, but the triumph of Newton's physics over Descartes was taken to be a triumph of empiricism over a priorism. From then, despite Kant's valiant attempt at reconciliation, a priorist methodologies have grown increasingly estranged from science. That left humane studies and social studies as fields to continue the struggle between the rivals. Simmel (1950), Durkheim (1938) and Weber (1949) all wrote their classics on the philosophy of the social sciences when the anti-science tendencies in German academic philosophy were at their peak. History done on Hegelian lines was the model for humanities and their a priorism was now known as hermeneutics. Both empiricism and a priorism are present in these classics.

The twentieth-century high tide of militant empiricism was the logical positivism movement that began in the 1920s. It appropriated all cognition into science, the success of which was attributed to the use of the empirical method. Theories not empirically verifiable were declared nonscientific and merely metaphysical. The battle line the positivists drew in social studies was, could the social sciences live up to their name by producing verifiable theories? If so, then the unity and identity of science and cognition could be upheld. In face of this challenge the a priorists took some time to regroup. Some, amazingly, retreated to the rather unpromising ground of Marxism (the Frankfurt School), which they tried to Hegelianize and a priorize (Frisby, 1976).

The primary interests of the logical positivists were in the natural sciences, but their predilection for a hodgepodge of logic, economics, statistics, Marx (note again how he confuses all issues), psychoanalysis and linguistics ensured that attempts were made to give a positivist account of them that would secure their place in unified science.

So long as logical positivism flourished within philosophy (down to the early 1960s), intense debates took place over the degree to which the empirical method could be utilized in what were now unselfconsciously called 'the social sciences'. The limits of mathematical and quantitative methods and simplicity were explored, as was the problem of whether facts could be separated from values. If social phenomena resisted measurement and quantification, and if they were permeated by values, the verifiable empirical basis of the social sciences was undermined. Along with the classics, the literature generated in this period is the core of most readers and courses in philosophy of the social sciences.

Meanwhile, the regrouped opponents of logical positivism engaged with precisely the same problems. They considered the limits of empiricism to be much more severe, and the problem of values to be much more pervasive, however, than did the logical positivists. Indeed it was argued that the limits of empiricism were the limits of natural science. As for values, these were the tip of the iceberg. As soon as the conscious, self-conscious, meaning-generating, and reflexive activities of human beings were under study, a totally different order of things was involved, demanding a totally different approach. That approach involved historical imagination – *Verstehen* – which requires the scrutiny of texts (hermeneutics) and some phenomenological rather than any empirical method (Natanson, 1963; Schutz, 1962; Dallmayr and McCarthy, 1977).

Disguised under the dispute about method was another about aims. Social things being unlike natural things, it was possible that attempting to explain and predict them was not only erroneous but inappropriate. Followers of the later Wittgenstein went even further than the continental a priorists and used the patron saint of logical positivism's later work to develop a transcendental argument against the very possibility of a science of the social. Winch (1958) and Louch (1966), despite differences, converge on the idea that what makes social things social as opposed to inert are the meaning-generating activities of human beings which show themselves in rules of behaviour. Language, for example, is not random noises but patterns that make sense. Clearly such rules are not natural; rather they are activities that define and constitute human life together. We cannot then explain human conduct in the way we offer mechanical causal explanation in science, but only by mastering from the inside the rules in use and their degrees of freedom. People do social things for reasons, not in obedience to laws. The vast literature on Winch and on whether reasons are causes can be traced through *The Philosopher's Index*.

Methodological Differences, Rationality, Relativism

The logical positivists and their opponents agree in translating metaphysical and epistemological issues into methodology. They also agree on the pivotal role played for method by the possibility of human intervention, in particular that intervention which is an unintended consequence of having thoughts about society that alter people's behaviour. (Popper (1945) labels this the Oedipus effect, Merton (1957) labels it the self-fulfilling prophecy.) Both Marxists and conservatives like to play down the desirable or effective scope for intervention in society, but this argument traps them with their own theories. What is the purpose of theorizing about society if the best we can do to improve it is to let it alone? Moreover, how is that view to be sustained when adequate theorizing itself improves society? One reaction to this is to attribute a privileged status to theorizing, to see it as somehow underdetermined by the general processes of determinism in society. Efforts were made first by Marx and Durkheim, and then, under the label 'sociology of knowledge', by Mannheim, to connect forms of putative cognition with social forms, class interest and the like, meanwhile exempting from such determination the natural sciences and that theorizing itself (Mannheim, 1936). The 'strong programme' of the sociology of knowledge – first proposed by Merton, although he attributes it to Mannheim – embraces science and exempts nothing. This is supported by the idea that reality, especially what people take reality to be, is itself a social construction – an idea that may be ascribed to the school of phenomenology but which goes specifically to Berger and Luckmann (1966). This issue, however, gets debated directly rather than methodologically, with the marshalling of comparative evidence to show how reality can be constructed very differently in different times and places. (Radical psychological theorists – labelling theory, so-called – extended the argument to the boundary between normal and abnormal psychological states, suggesting that psychopathology too is a matter of convention.) Much of the evidence came from anthropology, which had described societies where world-views, counting the very categories of language and hence of reality, were different from ours. Reality seemed socially relative. Winch (1964) extended his earlier work in this direction, arguing that Evans-Pritchard's classic study of Azande witchcraft (1937) was conceptually confused in comparing magic to science. Battle was joined by the anthropologist Horton (and Finnegan, 1973) who had upheld the validity of such comparisons. He thus followed Gellner, the leading critic of the various sociological idealisms.

Anthropology also stimulated the overlapping and so-called rationality debate, another treatment of the issue of relativism. The search for a characterization of what constituted man's rationality stemmed from Aristotle's suggestion that it was rationality that set the human animal apart from other animals. Rationality was for long taken to mean reasoning, ratiocination, logic. Mill (1843) took it for granted that logic was the laws of the human mind. Anthropologists had once held that uncivilized peoples lacked the ability to reason, were incapable, even, of coherent speech. In our century they reversed themselves and found primitive peoples to be as rational, if not in some ways more rational, than us. Yet their societies were without science and full of superstition, making them by positivist standards (logic and empiricism) not rational. Relativists argued that standards of rationality were embodied in differing social arrangements and hence differed. Absolutists argued that a necessary minimum for rationality – logic – was a necessary minimum for social life to function at all; therefore no societies were not rational. Still others tried to model degrees of rationality (Wilson, 1970; Jarvie, 1984). Recent developments, as we shall see, reveal new vigour among the relativists.

Logical positivism in philosophy petered out in the 1960s. The social sciences lagged a little behind. Political science and psychology experienced in the 1950s the 'behavioural revolution' (hence 'behavioural sciences' was a briefly fashionable name), in which positivist notions of aims and methods came to dominate – just as the positivist hegemony over philosophy was crumbling. More subtly, in sociology and anthropology the early positivism and empiricism of Durkheim had been blended in the 1940s into structural-functionalism, a way of going about thinking about society that, despite serious logical flaws (Gellner, 1973), survives in a modified form as the mainstream account of aims and methods. Although there was much debate about functionalism, it was endorsed as a method, perhaps because, stemming from a richer positivism, the extreme naturalism and inductivism of logical positivism rarely infected the work of sociologists and anthropologists – even if, sometimes, they echoed the rhetoric (Jarvie, 1964).

Already in the 1940s there had been intervention in the debates about the aims and methods of the social sciences from another quarter. An economist, Hayek, and an anti-positivist philosopher, Popper, in articles that became new classics as books (Hayek, 1952; Popper, 1957), argued that social scientists harboured mistaken views about the natural sciences. Hayek stressed that in science there were elements of a priori model building; Popper said that scientific method was trial and error. They thus criticized the identification of science with the positivist description of it. Both attacked the search for historical laws. Positivism was declared caricature and labelled 'scientism', then diagnosed as underlying the spurious claims not only of Marxists and positivists, but also as being what the continental a priorists were against.

Drawing primarily on the neglected example of economics, Hayek and Popper argued that the test of methods was results: by that test the freedom economists excercised to invent simplified models and work out their implications before complicating the models with real-world additions was one used generally in common sense and professional social thought. Their work was part of a vigorous methodological debate within economics stemming from Robbins (1932) and Hutchison (1938), later pressed further by Friedman (1953), Klappholz and Agassi (1959), and others. Alas, to the other social sciences economics is like mathematics to the nonscientist: a basic subject everyone knows they should be conversant with, and about which they feel guilty because they are ignorant of it. Moreover, there is ambivalence: economics has high status, yet whether economic theories are testable has been repeatedly questioned and still is. Hence the debates about model-building, rationality, realistic assumptions, whether theories should aim at truth or predictive success, and the value of mathematization that go on in economics (Boland, 1982) are scarcely referred to in discussions of the aims and methods of the other social sciences. This is especially poignant, because the debates within economics presuppose that economic behaviour is conventional and hence that the methods of economics are free to be different from those of natural science.

The very important point about false images of science shared by positivists, Marxists and anti-science a priorists had little impact. With the correction made, Hayek and Popper argued that simple modifications of method would allow the social sciences to belong to unified science. Moreover, the same modifications have to be made in cybernetics, which belongs to hard science – mathematics and engineering. Instead, the most controverted point was an ontological one. First, do humans act rationally – do they act at all? In opposition to the Hegelian tendency in Marx to reify abstractions and endow them with causal force (relations of production, classes, and so on), Hayek and Popper side-stepped ontology and proposed the principle of rational action or methodological individualism as more fruitful and in better conformity to the actual practice of the social sciences. This was the principle to attribute aims only to individuals and not to social wholes. Social institutions, they held, were real, but they were built, sustained and given aims only by individuals. A lively and extended debate continues (O'Neill, 1973).

To a large extent Popper and Hayek did not carry the day, as positivist and behavourist and holistic social science flourished through the 1960s. Early in that decade an essay on the history of science was published that was destined finally to purge logical positivism from the social sciences and yet which, like Popper, Hayek and the positivists, continued to urge the unity of science, while explicitly patronizing the social sciences as underdeveloped and hence not yet admissible. Its author, a physicist, was a self-taught historian utterly innocent of economics, sociology or any of the social sciences. The book was *The Structure of Scientific Revolutions*, the author, Thomas Kuhn (Barnes, 1982).

Kuhn argued that what distinguished a science from a prescience or a nonscience was its domination by a paradigm, that is, a recognized piece of work in the field that people copy in method, style and substance. In science such paradigms are fully in place when they are incorporated in current standard textbooks and imposed on novices. Noticing the incessant warring about fundamentals in the social sciences, the existence of rival textbooks, Kuhn could not but characterize them as presciences. There is some irony in the way social scientists have seized on Kuhn's ideas and reversed them, arguing that since the social sciences have textbooks they have paradigms, therefore they are sciences. But Kuhn specifically says there must be agreement amongst the leadership of a field on a single paradigm if that field is to count as scientific. Conclusion: there are as many social sciences, or branches of the social sciences, as there are paradigmatic works; once we declare that Freud and Piaget do not contest child psychology but that there are two fields, developmental psychology and cognitive psychology, a prescientific field is transformed into two paradigm-dominated and scientific fields.

Once again the debate has been vigorous. Kuhn's critics have argued that textbooks are also possessed by pseudoscience (astrology), nonscience (theology) and doubtful cases (psychoanalysis). More telling, Kuhn provides a legitimation-procedure for the boundary-drawing of academic bureaucrats who wish to conceal debate, controversy and confusion and give the impression of the orderly march of progress in 'fields', 'subjects', 'areas', and so on. Yet the categories of natural and conventional, not to mention physical, chemical, biological, or mathematical, may themselves stem from problems and hotly-debated theories (Hattiangadi, 1978/9).

A more relativist reading of Kuhn is that no special aims or methods characterize natural science, which is a subject much like any other, distinguishable if at all by its social status. Hence comparison with the social sciences was an empirical matter *for the social sciences* and the 'strong programme' of the sociology of knowledge vindicated itself (Bloor, 1976). Whether the results point to identity or contrast, they belong to the sociology of knowledge, which thus is the truly comprehensive discipline. Social studies of science, then, under whatever rubric, have implications in all directions, in sociology as well as philosophy, in metatheory as well as theory.

I. C. Jarvie
York University, Downsview, Ontario

References

Barnes, B. (1982), *T. S. Kuhn and Social Science*, London.

Berger, P. and Luckmann, T. (1966), *The Social Construction of Reality*, New York.

Bloor, D. (1976), *Knowledge and Social Imagery*, London.

Boland, L. A. (1982), *The Foundations of Economic Method*, London.

Dallmayr, F. and McCarthy, T. (1977), *Understanding Social Inquiry*, Washington.

Dijksterhuis, E. J. (1961), *The Mechanization of the World Picture*, New York.

Durkheim, E. (1938 [1895]), *Rules of Sociological Method*, Glencoe, Ill. (Original French, *Les Règles de la méthode sociologique*, Paris.)

Evans-Pritchard, E. E. (1937), *Witchcraft, Oracles and Magic Among the Azande*, Oxford.

Friedman, M. (1953), *Essays in Positive Economics*, Chicago.

Frisby, D. (ed.) (1976), *The Positivist Dispute in German Sociology*, London.

Gellner, E. (1973), *Cause and Meaning in the Social Sciences*, London.

Hattiangadi, J. N. (1978/9), 'The structure of problems: I and II', *Philosophy of the Social Sciences*, 8 and 9.

Hayek, F. A. (1952), *The Counter-Revolution of Science*, Glencoe. Ill.

Horton, W. R. and Finnegan, R. (eds) (1973), *Modes of Thought*, London.

Hutchison, T. W. (1938), *The Significance and Basic Postulates of Economic Theory*, London.

Jarvie, I. C. (1964), *The Revolution in Anthropology*, London.

Jarvie, I. C. (1984), *Rationality and Relativism*, London.

Kaufmann, F. (1944), *Methodology of the Social Sciences*, Oxford.

Klappholz, K. and Agassi, J. (1959), 'Methodological prescriptions in economics', *Economica*, 26.

Kuhn, T. S. (1962), *The Structure of Scientific Revolutions*, Chicago.

Louch, A. R. (1966), *Explanation and Social Action*, Berkeley and Los Angeles.

Mannheim, K. (1936 [1929]), *Ideology and Utopia*, London. (Original German, *Ideologie und Utopie*, Bonn.)

Merton, R. (1957), *Social Theory and Social Structure*, Glencoe, Ill.

Mill, J. S. (1843), *A System of Logic*, London.

Natanson, M. (ed.) (1963), *Philosophy of the Social Sciences: A Reader*, New York.

O'Neill, J. (ed.) (1973), *Modes of Individualism and Collectivism*, London.

Popper, K. R. (1945), *The Open Society and Its Enemies*, London.

Popper, K. R. (1957), *The Poverty of Historicism*, London.

Robbins, L. (1932), *Essay on the Nature and Significance of Economic Science*, London.

Schutz, A. (1962), *Collected Papers*, Vol. I: *The Problem of Social Reality*, The Hague.

Simmel, G. (1950), *The Sociology of Georg Simmel*, ed. K. H. Wolff, Glencoe, Ill.

Weber, M. (1949), *Methodology of the Social Sciences*, ed. E. Shils, Glencoe, Ill.

Wilson, B. (ed.) (1970), *Rationality*, Oxford.

Winch, P. (1958), *The Idea of a Social Science*, London.

Winch, P. (1964), 'Understanding a primitive society', *American Philosophical Quarterly*, 1.

Further Reading

Agassi, J. (1960), 'Methodological individualism', in O'Neill (1973).

Agassi, J. (1975), 'Institutional individualism,' *British Journal of Sociology*, 26.

Aggasi, J. (1977), *Towards a Rational Philosophical Anthropology*, The Hague.

Bhaskar, R. (1979), *The Possibility of Naturalism: A Philosophical Critique of the Contemporary Social Sciences*, Brighton.

Borger, R. and Cioffi, F. (1970), *Explanation in the Behavioural Sciences*, Cambridge.

Brodbeck, M. (ed.) (1968), *Readings in the Philosophy of the Social Sciences*, New York.

Brown, R. (1963), *Explanation in Social Science*, London.

Brown, S. C. (ed.) (1979), *Philosophical Disputes in the Social Sciences*, Brighton.

Collingwood, R. G. (1946), *The Idea of History*, Oxford.

Dixon, K. (1973), *Sociological Theory: Pretence and Possibility*, London.

Durkheim, E. (1915 [1912]), *Elementary Forms of the Religious Life*, London. (Original French, *Les Formes élémentaires de la vie religieuse*, Paris.)

Emmet, D. and MacIntyre, A. (1970), *Sociological Theory and Philosophical Analysis*, London.

Feigl, H. and Brodbeck, M. (1953), *Readings in the Philosophy of Science*, New York.

Gellner, E. (1964), *Thought and Change*, London.

Gellner, E. (1980), *Spectacles and Predicaments*, Cambridge.

Giddens, A. (1976), *New Rules of Sociological Method*, New York.

Hollis, M. and Lukes, S. (eds) (1982), *Rationality and Relativism*, Oxford.

Hookway, C. and Pettit, P. (eds) (1978), *Action and Interpretation*, Cambridge.

Jarvie, I. C. (1972), *Concepts and Society*, London.

Krimerman, L. (ed.), *The Nature and Scope of Social Science. A Critical Anthology*, New York.

Simmel, G. (1959), *Essays on Sociology, Philosophy and Aesthetics*, New York.

Simmel, G. (1980), *Essays on Interpretation in Social Science*, Totowa.

See also: *Habermas; Kuhn; Popper; positivism; relativism.*

Bayes' Theorem

Bayes' Theorem is an elementary result in the theory of probability named after the Reverend Thomas Bayes, an English Presbyterian minister who, in a posthumously published essay (Bayes, 1764), first presented a special case of it, and proposed its use in statistical inference. When viewed as part of probability theory, Bayes' Theorem is a simple rule for computing the conditional probability of each of a set of k mutually exclusive and exhaustive events $H_1, H_2, \ldots, H_k$, when an event E is given:

$$\Pr(H_i|E) = \frac{\Pr(H_i)\Pr(E|H_i)}{\sum\limits_{j=1}^{k} \Pr(H_j)\Pr(E|H_j)} \quad i = 1,2, \ldots, k.$$

Here $\Pr(H_i)$ is the *prior* probability of the event H_i, and $\Pr(E|H_i)$ is the conditional probability of the event E given that H_i has occurred or is true. The rule then gives the *posterior* probability of the event H_i given the occurrence of E, $P(H_i|E)$.

When Bayes' Theorem is used as the basis of statistical inference, the occurrence of E might correspond to the results of an experiment or the data from a sample survey, and the events $H_i, H_2, \ldots, H_k$ might correspond to competing hypotheses or to different values of a parameter in a statistical model. The difficulty that has prevented the use of Bayes' Theorem for virtually all statistical inference purposes is the determination of the *a priori* probabilities, $\Pr(H_i)$ for $i = 1,2,\ldots,k$. The lack of agreement regarding the values of these *a priori* probabilities has led many statisticians to turn to other modes of inference.

Bayesian inference or Bayesian statistics is an approach to

inference linked to the theory of subjective or personal probability, based on degrees of belief as opposed to being based only on long-run frequencies. Subject to formal rules of *coherence,* each individual assesses personal, *a priori* probabilities, $Pr(H_i)$, and updates them using the data via Bayes' Theorem to produce personal *a posteriori* probabilities. The rise of current interest in the subjective approach dates to the work of Bruno de Finetti in the 1930s, and Leonard J. Savage in the 1950s. Bayes' Theorem now plays, for many statisticians, the role in inference originally described in Thomas Bayes's historic essay.

Stephen E. Fienberg
Carnegie–Mellon University

Reference
Bayes, T. (1963 [1764]), *Facsimiles of Two Papers by Bayes,* New York.
See also: *statistical reasoning.*

Behaviourism

Behaviourism is mainly a twentieth-century orientation within the discipline of psychology in the United States. The behavioural approach emphasizes the objective study of the relationships between environmental manipulations and human and animal behaviour change, usually in laboratory or relatively controlled institutional settings. Emerging as a discrete movement just prior to World War I, behaviourism represented a vigorous rejection of psychology defined as the introspective study of the human mind and consciousness. Early behaviourists eschewed the structuralism of Wundt and Titchener, the functional mentalism of James, Dewey, Angell and Carr, and the relativism and phenomenology of Gestalt psychology.

John B. Watson is credited with declaring behaviourism a new movement in 1913; but the foundations of the development extend back to the ancient Greeks and include empiricism, elementism, associationism, objectivism and naturalism. The direct antecedents of of behaviourism during the late nineteenth and early twentieth centuries were: the studies of animal behaviour and the functional orientation inspired by Darwin's theory of evolution; the conditioning research of Russian physiologists Ivan Pavlov and Vladimir Bekhterev emphasizing stimulus substitution in the context of reflexive behaviour; and the puzzle-box studies of American psychologist Edward Thorndike concerned with the effects of the consequences of behaviour on response frequency. The two predominant and often competing theoretical-procedural models of conditioning research have been classical conditioning derived from the work of Pavlov and Bekhterev, and Skinner's operant conditioning.

While it is generally claimed that behaviourism as a distinct school ceased to exist by the 1950s, behaviourism as a general orientation has gone through the following overlapping periods: classical behaviourism (1900–25), represented by the work of Thorndike and Watson; neo-behaviourism (1920s–40s), an exciting time when the theories of Clark Hull, Edward Tolman, Edwin Guthrie and Burrhus F. Skinner competed for pre-eminence; Hullian behaviourism (1940s–50s) when Hull's complex hypothetico-deductive behaviour theory appeared most promising; Skinnerian behaviourism (1960s–mid-1970s) during which time operant conditioning techniques, emphasizing the control of behaviour implicit in the consequences of behaviour, afforded the most powerful methodologies; and finally cognitive behaviourism (1975–present) when the limits of a purely Skinnerian approach to behaviour change became increasingly apparent, and cognitive perspectives, such as social learning theories, seemed necessary to account for behaviour change.

A behavioural orientation has been central to twentieth-century psychology in the United States primarily because of a strong faith in laboratory research and experimental method-ologies; an interest in studying the process of learning; a prefer-ence for quantitative information; the elimination from the discipline of ambiguous concepts and investigations of complex and therefore difficult to describe private (subjective) experi-ences; and, since the late 1950s, a very conservative approach to theory building.

While each of the major behavioural programmes from Thorndike's to Skinner's failed to provide a comprehensive account of behaviour change, the behavioural orientation has led to the development of behaviour-control methodologies with useful application in most areas of psychology. In addition, the movement has inspired precision and accountability in psychological inquiry.

Behavioural methodologies have, of course, been employed by psychologists in countries other than the United States, particularly those with strong scientific traditions such as Britain and Japan. Behavioural assumptions have also influenced other social sciences, especially sociology and political science. But because laboratory animal research is central to the behavioural orientation, behaviourism as a major movement only developed in psychology.

Albert R. Gilgen
University of Northern Iowa

Further Reading
Marx, M. H. and Hillix, W. A. (1979), *Systems and Theories in Psychology*, New York.

Case Studies
Case studies are detailed perceptions of connected processes in individual and collective experience. They have the following distinctive features:
(1) They contain *cases*, instances of theoretical principles. Not every case need be typical, but 'ideal-typical' cases sometimes provide particularly 'apt illustrations' (Gluckman, 1961).
(2) They discuss *particularities*, including particular individuals (pseudonymized), rather than merely the abstracted roles of, for example, spouses. They carefully follow events such as those preceding particular divorces, particular strikes or particular development schemes before generalizing about incompatible conjugal roles, causes of industrial conflict or achievable policies. Data transcend analysis, inviting alternative interpretations.
(3) They are case *histories*, recording ongoing processes in the relationship between particular individuals, the interaction of particular individuals with particular institutions, the step-by-step transformation of particular institutions, the vicissitudes of

particular social movements faced with support or antagonism from particular individuals or groups, and so on. Because the same actors appear in diverse situations, defining or redefining their relationships, pursuing or resolving their conflicts, case studies have not been common in static structural-functional models, which divide the social universe into 'political', 'kinship', 'economic', and so on. However, Turner (1968) used case studies to investigate processes maintaining structural continuity, van Velsen (1967) stressed their indispensability in studying structural change, and Blau (1963) used them to demonstrate 'permanence of change' in bureaucracies regarded as structurally rigid.

(4) They are frequently *social-problem oriented*. Disputes are analysed long before they come to court – if they ever do. Case studies unearth processes which lead to some activities being labelled as social problems but which leave other activities, arguably more harmful, of little public interest. Case studies demonstrate the principle that issues alter as different groups adopt them. Thus, Spector and Kitsuse (1977) delineated how American concern for Soviet dissidents in mental hospitals was replaced by one related issue after another until the 'main' one became *American* psychiatrists' resistance to judicial cross-examination.

Methods

(1) All science involves comparison. Individual researchers may not arrange case studies comparatively themselves, preferring to detail a few cases. However, their cases and others' must be continually scrutinized for variables on which to base generalizations.

(2) Ongoing dialogue between conjecture and data-gathering attenuates distinctions between deduction and induction.

(3) Detail demands diverse techniques, including analysis of documents, both official and personal, taped interviews and informant feedback. Participant observation is particularly important, for casual conversation and observing people in 'unguarded moments' (Langness, 1970) often suggest fresh lines of investigation. Superficial rapport, however, can impair case-studies. Authenticity also requires cross-checking. Follow-up

and replication studies test whether developments in the short term continue in the long term, and whether developments in one set of circumstances are repeated in another.

(4) Writing up case studies itself deepens understanding. Familiar postulates often fail to do justice to complex information, making conceptual refinement necessary. Resulting 'sensitizing concepts', without masquerading as 'grand theory', enable other researchers to apply them to very different sociological problems. Even unconceptualized case studies, however, may bring conventional suppositions into question.

(5) Statistical inferences are derivable from case-study variables, although common sociological failings are absence of case studies *and* of quantitative estimation of variance (Rosenblatt, 1981). Unfortunately many statistical studies dispense with sensitizing concepts. Such studies seem unaware that 'more discoveries have arisen from intense observation than from statistics applied to large groups' (Beveridge, 1951). Eysenck, who once regarded case studies as mere anecdotage, now takes the view that 'We simply have to keep our eyes open and look carefully at individual cases – not in the hope of proving anything, but rather in the hope of learning something' (1976).

Maurice Glickman
University of Botswana

References

Beveridge, W. I. B. (1951), *The Art of Scientific Investigation*, London.

Blau, P. (1963), *The Dynamics of Bureaucracy: A Study of Interpersonal Relations in Two Government Agencies*, London.

Eysenck, H. (1976), 'Introduction', in *Case Studies in Behaviour Therapy*, London.

Gluckman, M. (1961), 'Ethnographic data in British social anthropology', *Sociological Review*, 9.

Langness, L. (1970), 'Unguarded moments', in R. Naroll and R. Cohen (eds), *A Handbook of Cultural Anthropology*, New York.

Rosenblatt, P. (1981), 'Ethnographic case studies', in M.

Brewer and B. Collins (eds), *Scientific Enquiry and the Social Sciences*, London.

Spector, M. and Kitsuse, J. (1977), *Constructing Social Problems*, London.

Turner, V. W. (1968), *Schism and Continuity in an African Society: A Study of Ndembu Village Life*, Manchester.

Van Velsen, J. (1967), 'The extended-case method and situational analysis', in A. L. Epstein (ed.), *The Craft of Social Anthropology*, London.

See also: *life histories*.

Catastrophe Theory

Historically the field of research known as catastrophe theory began with the ideas of the French topologist René Thom in the early 1960s. In purely mathematical terms, elementary catastrophe theory is concerned with the classification of singularities of differentiable mappings on manifolds. A catastrophe is a singularity in a map that arises stably in the following way. Let C be an n-dimensional control or parameter space, let X be a k-dimensional behaviour or state space, and let f be a smooth generic potential-like function on X parametrized by the manifold C. Let M be the set of stationary values of f obtained by setting the partial derivatives of f with respect to the coordinates x_i of X equal to zero. Then M is a smooth surface or hypersurface (the catastrophe manifold). Regions on M represent maximum or minimum values of the potential function f. A catastrophe is a structurally stable singularity of the projection of M onto the control space C.

If the number of dimensions n of the control space is 4 or less, there are only 7 elementary catastrophes.

Catastrophe theory provides a coherent framework for modelling the complex dynamics of systems. Points on the catastrophe manifold represent stationary values of the potential-like function associated with the behaviour of the system. The position of the state point on the manifold is determined by combinations of the control variables or factors. Smooth, continuous changes in the control factors can result in qualitatively distinct types of behaviour of the state point. It may move in a smooth, continuous trajectory along the surface of the manifold.

| Elementary catastrophes | | Dimension | Dimension |
Family	Name	of X	of C
Cuspoids	Fold	1	1
	Simple cusp	1	2
	Swallowtail	1	3
	Butterfly	1	4
Umbilics	Hyperbolic	2	3
	Elliptic	2	3
	Parabolic	2	4

However, smooth changes in the control factors may also cause a sudden, discontinuous ('catastrophic') jump of the state point from one region of the catastrophe manifold to another. Thus by means of catastrophe theory one is able to model the smooth, continuous processes of change and development, as well as the occurrence of phenomena associated with the dynamics of instability within the same framework.

Applications of catastrophe theory divide into two distinct categories. On the one hand, there is an expanding corpus of successful studies concerned with rigorous applications of the formal mathematical theory. The applications are largely in physics and engineering (Poston and Stewart, 1978; Gilmore, 1981, and some of the examples in Zeeman, 1977). The aim is utilitarian and oriented towards the quantitative analysis of specified dynamic systems. On the other hand, the approach exemplified by the work of Thom is essentially hermeneutic and interpretative. The interest is in providing a global, qualitative view of the dynamics of a system. One postulates the applicability of some elementary catastrophe as a model for the system of interest, and analyses its dynamics in terms of the properties of the model. Applications of catastrophe model building are found in biology and the social sciences (Thom, 1976, 1983; Zeeman, 1977).

Franklin E. Tjon Sie Fat
University of Leiden

References
Gilmore, R. (1981), *Catastrophe Theory for Scientists and Engineers*, New York.
Poston, T. and Stewart, I. (1978), *Catastrophe Theory and its Applications*, London.
Thom, R. (1976), *Structural Stability and Morphogenesis. An Outline of a General Theory of Models*, Reading, Mass.
Thom, R. (1983), *Mathematical Models of Morphogenesis*, Chichester.
Zeeman, E. C. (1977), *Catastrophe Theory. Selected Papers 1972–1977*, Reading, Mass.

Further Reading
Behavioral Science (1978), 23, Special issue on applications of catastrophe theory in the behavioral and life sciences.
Deakin, M. A. B. (1980), 'Applied catastrophe theory in the social and biological sciences', *Bulletin of Mathematical Biology*, 42.

Categorical Data
Definition and Notation
Categorical data in its broadest sense is simply a collection of values of discrete variables obtained from a sample of individuals or objects. Here the term discrete variable means a variable which can have only a finite number of values (levels or categories). These levels may also have other features, such as a natural order.

A common type of categorical data arises if the same p variables $X_1, X_2, \ldots, X_p$ (say) are measured on each individual. In this case, a convenient means of summarizing the resulting data is in the form of a p-way contingency table. Such a table gives the number of individuals with any given configuration of values of the p discrete variables. If $n_1, n_2, \ldots, n_p$ denote the number of categories of each of the variables, then the contingency table will have $n_1 \times n_2 \times \ldots \times n_p$ entries (or cells). Table 1, which combines tables 5.3–1 and 5.3–5 in Bishop, Fienberg and Holland (1975), illustrates a three-way contingency table.

As an example, the number 320 in Table 1 shows that there were 320 father-son pairs in the sample who were British and

Table 1 Social mobility data

Country	Father's status	Son's status				
		1	2	3	4	5
Britain	1	50	45	8	18	8
	2	28	174	84	154	55
	3	11	78	110	223	96
	4	14	150	185	714	447
	5	0	42	72	320	411
Denmark	1	18	17	16	4	2
	2	24	105	109	59	21
	3	23	84	289	217	95
	4	8	49	175	348	198
	5	6	8	69	201	246

had status levels 5 and 4 respectively. The status categories have a natural order (and are said to be ordinal), whereas the country categories have no natural order (and hence have a nominal scale).

If there are variables measured on some but not all individuals, the data is not representable as a contingency table unless extra categories are invented to denote missing values of variables. (Having said this, the discussion will be restricted to categorical data *naturally* summarized by a contingency table.)

The following notation and conventions will be used throughout: Given a finite number of discrete variables $(X_1, X_2, X_3, \ldots)$ measured on a sample of individuals, the symbol $n_{ijk\ldots}$ stands for the number of individuals with $X_1 = i$, $X_2 = j$, $X_3 = k, \ldots$ The corresponding expected count under a given model is denoted by $m_{ijk\ldots}$ and $p_{ijk\ldots} = $ Probability $(X_1 = i, X_2 = j, X_3 = k, \ldots) > 0$. A plus sign $(+)$ used as a subscript denotes summation over an index e.g. $p_{i+k} = \sum_j p_{ijk}$. To avoid technical problems, all divisors in mathematical expressions will be assumed to be positive. Finally, the symbol ln is used to denote the natural (base e) logarithm.

Sampling Assumptions

Basic to any analysis of categorical data is a consideration of how the data was (or is to be) collected. This is essential in the formulation of an appropriate statistical model for the data.

As an illustration of different sampling schemes and possible models, consider Table 1. One way in which the data could have been collected is by determining *beforehand* the number of father-son pairs in Britain and in Denmark to be surveyed. In this situation, a suitable model for the distribution of the counts n_{ijk} ($X_1 =$ Country, $X_2 =$ Father's status, $X_3 =$ Son's status) might be a product of two multinomials, one for the counts obtained in Britain and one for those obtained in Denmark. These multinomials would have sample sizes n_{i++} and probabilities $\{p_{ijk} = m_{ijk}/n_{i++}; j,k = 1, \ldots, 5\}$ for $i = 1$ (Britain) and 2 (Denmark) respectively.

An alternative way in which the data could have been obtained is by interviewing as many pairs in Britain and Denmark as was possible within a fixed time period or budget. In this case the total sample size in each country would be random, and a suitable model for the counts in Table 1 might be the product of all values of i,j,k of Poisson distributions of the form

$$\{\exp(-m_{ijk}) \; (m_{ijk})^{n_{ijk}}\}n/_{ijk}!$$

where exp denotes the exponential function and $n! = n(n - 1) \ldots 1$.

For further discussion concerning sampling distributions, in particular product multinomial and Poisson models, see Bishop, Fienberg and Holland (1975). It should be emphasized that how closely the data conforms with any distributional assumptions is a matter which requires checking.

Log-Linear Models

Statistical models for contingency tables generally consist of two parts. The first part involves the specification of a probability distribution for the counts in the table, and this has been mentioned in Section 2 above. The second part involves formulating a suitable structure for the expected counts, relating them to the levels of the discrete variables. The suitability of any given structure at this second stage will depend on a knowledge of the sampling scheme and whether some variable(s) is (are) considered *response variables* and the rest *explanatory*. Of the many possibilities, the discussion below is limited to a particular type of *log-linear* model for the expected counts, one which can be used to express hypotheses concerning *interaction* (association) between variables as well as *conditional independence* relations. In doing so, the implicit assumption is made that the table has no *structural zeros*, i.e. there are no cells with zero probability of having a positive count. It is important to recognize structural zeros in a table if they exist (see Bishop, Fienberg and Holland, 1975; Fienberg, 1977).

The type of log-linear model to be considered here expresses the natural logarithm of the expected counts as a linear function of *interaction* or *association terms*. An example of such a model for Table 1 is

$$\ln m_{ik} = u + u_{1(i)} + u_{2(j)} + u_{3(k)} + u_{12(ij)} + u_{13(ik)} + u_{23(jk)}^{(1)} + u_{123(ijk)}.$$

The term $u_{1(i)}$ denotes the main (or zero order interaction) effect of X_1 when it is at level i, $u_{12(ij)}$ denotes the first order interaction effect of variable X_1 and X_2 when they are at levels i and j respectively, while $u_{123(ijk)}$ denotes the second order interaction effect of variables X_1, X_2, X_3 when they are at levels i,j,k respectively. All the u-terms in (1) satisfy the usual analysis of variance type constraints that the sum over any subscript within a bracket is zero e.g. $\Sigma u_{23(jk)} = \xi_k u_{23(jk)} = 0$. For an interpretation of the u-parameters in terms of measures of association, in particular cross-product ratios, see Bishop, Fienberg and Holland (1975). In general a p-way contingency table can have interaction terms up to order $p - 1$.

Equation (1) is an example of a *saturated* log-linear model i.e. one which allows all possible interaction terms. As such it imposes no constraints on the expected counts. An example of a non-saturated model is when $u_{123(ijk)} = u_{12(ij)} = u_{13(ik)} = u_{23(jk)} = 0$ in (1). This corresponds to the hypothesis of no interaction effects or, under a product multinomial sampling scheme for Table 1, the conditional independence of the two status variables given country of origin.

A log-linear model of the type above is said to be *hierarchical* if it has the property that whenever an interaction term involving a set B of variables is in the model then so are all the interaction terms involving subsets of B. There are difficulties in interpreting these models when they are not hierarchical (see for example Fienberg, 1977).

A shorthand way of specifying a hierarchical log-linear model is by giving its *generating class*, or, in the terminology of Bishop, Fienberg and Holland (1975), the set of minimal sufficient configurations. The generating class identifies the maximal order interaction terms in the model and can be used to write down all the model terms. This is illustrated in Example 1 below.

Example 1. Suppose the generating class of a log-linear model for a four-way table is given to be [123], [24], [34]. This means that $u_{123(ijk)}$, $u_{24(jl)}$ and $u_{34(kl)}$ are in the model and consequently all the terms in Equation (1) as well as u, $u_{(2j)}$, $u_{4(1)}$, $u_{24(jl)}$, and u, $u_{3(k)}$, $u_{4(1)}$, $u_{34(kl)}$. Adding all these, including any term only once, gives us the form of the model.

As has been alluded to earlier, certain log-linear models can be interpreted in terms of conditional independence constraints imposed on the variables. For multinomial sampling models it is possible to summarize conveniently the conditional independence relations (if any) implied by a given log-linear model by associating it with a graph. Details can be found in Kiiveri and Speed (1982) and Darroch, Lauritzen and Speed (1980).

Additional information can be used to improve the analysis of a contingency table. One form of additional information not utilized in the discussion so far is ordering of the levels of one or more of the discrete variables. (See Fienberg (1977) for an example and discussion of a model incorporating such information.)

Models which explicity make use of the fact that one variable is a response and the others explanatory can be found in Fienberg (1977) and Haberman (1978; 1979).

Estimation and Goodness-of-Fit

The u-parameters in log-linear models or equivalently the expected counts can be estimated using maximum likelihood methods. An important result concerning these estimates is that they are the same for product multinomial and the simpler Poisson likelihoods *provided* all u-terms involving variables with margins fixed beforehand are included in the log-linear model (See Bishop, Fienberg and Holland, 1975).

To test the goodness of fit of a particular log-linear model either of the following statistics could be used:

$$X^2 = \sum_{i,j,k,\ldots} (\hat{m}_{ink\ldots} - n_{ijk\ldots})2/\hat{m}_{ijk\ldots} \quad (2)$$

$$G^2 = 2\sum_{i,j,k,\ldots} \hat{m}_{ijk\ldots} \ln(\hat{m}_{ijk\ldots}/n_{ijk\ldots}) \quad (3)$$

where $\hat{m}_{ijk\ldots}$ is the estimated expected count under the model. Both statistics have an asymptotic chi-square distribution with degrees of freedom equal to the total number of cells in the table minus the total number of parameters in the model. Computation of the degrees of freedom is more difficult if the table has structural zeroes (Haberman, 1978). The likelihood-ratio statistic (3) has the attractive property that it can be partitioned into a number of additive components for a nested hierachy of models (see Fienberg, 1977).

Procedures useful for isolating counts with undue influence on estimates, systematic departures from log-linearity and the like can be found in Pregibon (1981).

Other Topics

Some topics of special interest to social scientists, namely causal models for systems of discrete variables and latent class models, have been omitted. References which can be consulted for further information regarding these are Kiiveri and Speed (1982), Goodman (1978) and Haberman (1979).

H. T. Kiiveri
CSIRO Institute of
Physical Sciences, Australia

References

Bishop, Y. M. M., Fienberg, S. E. and Holland, P. W. (1975), *Discrete Multivariate Analysis: Theory and Practice*, Cambridge, Mass.

Darroch, J. N., Lauritzen, S. L. and Speed, T. P. (1980), 'Log-linear models for contingency tables and Markov fields over graphs', *Annals of Statistics*, 8.

Fienberg, S. E. (1977), *The Analysis of Cross-Classified Categorical Data*, Cambridge, Mass.

Goodman, L. A. (1978), *Analyzing Qualitative Categorical Data: Log-linear Models and Latent Struture Analysis*, ed. J. Magidson, Cambridge, Mass.

Haberman, S. J. (1978), *Analysis of Qualitative Data, Volume 1: Introductory Topics*, New York.

Haberman, S. J. (1979), *Analysis of Qualitative Data, Volume 2: New Developments*, New York.

Kiiveri, H. T. and Speed, T. P. (1982), 'Structural analysis of multivariate data: a review', in S. Leinhardt (ed.), *Sociological Methodology 1982*, San Francisco.

Pregibon, D. (1981), 'Logistic regression diagnostics', *Annals of Statistics*, 9.

See also: *multivariate analysis*.

Computer Simulation

Computer simulation is a methodology for building, testing, and using computer programs which imitate (latin *simulare*, to imitate) system behaviour. Numbers or symbols representing a system and its parts are stored in computer memory and are manipulated by a *simulation program* written in a suitable computer programming language.

A useful approach to simulation modelling is the so-called *entity-attribute-relationship* approach. A system is thought of as a collection of one or more entities each of which has one or more attributes. In addition, various relationships exist between the entities. As time passes, activities or events occur in the system to cause entities to be created or destroyed, or to undergo changes in their attributes or relationships to other entities. Most simulation models in the social sciences can be formulated using the entity-attribute-relationship approach.

When the entire system is treated as a single entity, the simulation model is called a *macro-simulation*. For example, an entire population might be simulated as one entity with attributes representing the numbers of people in various categories within the population. The simulation program would change these numbers from one simulated time period to the next in order to imitate the processes of birth, death, marriage, migration, etc., in the real population. Macro-simulation models can usually be represented by systems of equations which are solvable by traditional mathematical methods, but which require computer simulation for practical reasons.

When a system is treated as a collection of many entities which, taken as a whole, make up the system, then the simulation model is called a *micro-simulation*. For example, each person in a population might be modelled as an entity with attributes of age, sex, marital status, and so on. The simulation program would cause each entity (person) to experience events such as birth, marriage, and death at appropriate times during the course of the simulation. At any time during the simulation, features of the population, such as the number of people with a given age and marital status, could be obtained by simply counting the appropriate entities. Micro-simulation models are often difficult to represent with traditional mathematical notation, and it is for these types of models that computer simulation methods are most often used in the social sciences.

Most micro-simulation models are *stochastic* models in the sense that some degree of randomness is allowed in the behaviour of individual entities. In a simulation program *pseudo-random numbers* are used to simulate randomness. Strictly speaking, computers cannot generate truly random numbers, but methods for generating pseudo-random numbers with most of the important properties of true random numbers are well developed. By using the *inverse transform method*, pseudo-random numbers representing a wide range of probability distributions can be generated as needed during the course of a simulation. Stochastic micro-simulations are also called *monte-carlo simulations* because of their reliance upon random numbers.

A critical and often slighted task in computer simulation modelling is that of program *verification*. This is the process of determining that the simulation program does not contain logical errors which could lead to meaningless results. Verification of stochastic simulations is especially difficult, since some logical errors may be evident only when certain rare events, or rare combinations of events, occur during the course of a simulation. But by keeping simulation models as simple as possible, by testing with fixed extreme values in place of pseudo-random numbers, and by spending ample time verifying the program, reliable stochastic simulation programs can be produced.

Validation is the process of comparing simulation results to empirical data in order to determine whether the simulation program imitates the real system closely enough for its intended purposes. Standard statistical procedures are used to determine whether results from stochastic simulations differ from empirical data by a significant amount. *Tuning* a simulation model involves making necessary adjustments to achieve a desired degree of validity. Like any scientific model, a simulation model is a simplified representation of reality and is not intended to match perfectly the behaviour of the real system. Therefore, model validity can only be judged relative to the particular research context.

Sometimes the emphasis in simulation modelling is on *prediction*, while at other times it is on *sensitivity analysis*. The former involves interpreting simulation results as statements about actual past, present, or future system behaviour. Predictions derived from computer simulation models are prone to the same errors as other types of predictions, and in most social science, applications have proven less than adequately accurate. Sensitivity analysis refers to the use of a simulation model to explore the response of selected output variables to specified changes in system parameters or input variables. The emphasis is on understanding the behavioural dynamics of a system rather than upon predicting its behaviour. The general trend is toward this use of computer simulation.

Because they include a random component, stochastic simulations yield information about *variances* as well as *expected values* of simulation results. Each repeated execution of a simulation program, or *replication*, produces results that differs from the results of other replications due to the random component. All of the replications necessary to answer a particular research question constitute a *simulation experiment*, and the principles of experimental design apply to the design of efficient and informative simulation experiments with the added advantage that the nature of the random component can be controlled by the experimenter.

The practice of computer simulation is closely tied to the technology of computing. The early micro-simulation experiments of Orcutt *et al.* (1961) consumed vast amounts of computer time on a large computer that was slower and had less memory than today's inexpensive microcomputers. But even with advanced technology, computer simulation typically requires large amounts of computing resources, largely due to the need for many replications in most simulation experiments. The task of simulation programming is greatly simplified by specialized programming languages which provide for automatic memory management for large numbers of entities, the timing of events during the course of the simulation, and the generation of pseudo-random numbers. Many elementary texts (for example, Mitrani 1982; Payne 1982) introduce the concepts, issues, and programming languages relevant to computer simulation.

James E. Smith
Cambridge Group for the History
of Population and Social Structure

References

Mitrani, I. (1982), *Simulation Techniques for Discrete Event Systems*, Cambridge.

Orcutt, G. H., Greenberger, M., Korbel, J. and Rivlin, A. M. (1961), *Microanalysis of Socioeconomic Systems: A Simulation Study*, New York.

Payne, J. A. (1982), *Introduction to Simulation: Programming Techniques and Methods of Analysis*, New York.

Ethics in Social Research

Social research ethics involve the consideration of the moral implications of social science inquiry. Ethics is a matter of principled sensitivity to the rights of others, in such a way that human beings who are being studied by social scientists are treated as ends rather than as means. Such ethical issues frequently also lead to consideration of the politics of research, the place of the investigator in the power structure, and the wider social impact of research. Those conducting social research need increasingly to be aware of the ethical and political implications of their actions.

The protection of human subjects is enshrined in the doctrine of informed consent, first developed in biomedical research. This stipulates that the voluntary consent of the human subject is essential, and this should be freely given without duress, and knowing and understanding what the research involves. Most social research, whether by experimental, social survey or observational methods, respects this principle, but there have been occasional sharp controversies where experimental or observational subjects have been left in ignorance of research, or have had research misrepresented to them. In observing the principle, most social scientists do not follow the formal procedures used in medical research such as signed consent forms.

A related controversy has concerned the use of deception in social research. The majority of social scientists are open about their purposes and aims, but in rare cases deception has been used on the grounds that, because of practical methodological or moral considerations, research could not otherwise be carried out. (Such studies include research on obedience to authority, and sexual deviance.) Objections to deception include its degrading and false character, its harmful social consequences, harm to the investigator, the creation of suspicion among subjects, and the breach of informed consent.

Research may in certain circumstances impinge upon the privacy of research subjects (that is, the freedom of the individual to decide how much of the self to reveal to others, when and to whom). Some information about the individual may be sensitive. Some settings (for example, jury rooms, Cabinet meetings) may be entirely closed to outsiders. The wider dissemination of research results may affect subjects adversely. Such problems may be handled by obtaining informed consent or by various forms of making data anonymous. In the latter case, for example, the location in which research was carried out may be concealed and the identities of particular individuals hidden under pseudonyms. A distinction may be made between the circumstances under which data are collected, and their subsequent storage, dissemination, analysis and re-analysis. Issues of confidentiality are raised by the latter, though also impinging upon collection. What will happen to data once collected? To whom will they be available? What repercussions might there be for the individual in providing certain data to a social researcher?

The importance of these questions has been intensified by the advent of the electronic computer, with immensely powerful means of large-scale data storage and retrieval. This has a major impact upon census data and large-scale social survey data. Various techniques have been developed to ensure that individual identities cannot be linked to published information. These include the deletion of individual identifiers such as name, address or local area of residence; the suppression of tables containing small numbers of cases; and processes of random error injection. In addition to physical security, technical means exist for making anonymous the data held in computer files, including the separation of identifiers from the main body of data and their linkage by suitable codes. Randomized response is a method of ensuring the confidentiality of data while it is being collected.

The ethical issues raised by research go wider than the treatment of research subjects and handling of data once collected. The social impact of research has been of concern and controversy both within particular societies (as in the Moynihan Report on Black families in the US) and internationally (as in Project Camelot in Chile in the 1960s). There is increasing concern about the sponsorship of research (who pays? for whom, and in whose interest, is research conducted?), the negotiation of research access (especially the role played by gatekeepers, who may give or withhold permission), and about the possible adverse effects of the publication of research results on certain weaker groups or lower status sections of society. The investigator can rarely control any of these factors, but awareness of them can help to produce more effective work. Particular care is also required to review the ethical implications of action research and applied research leading to social intervention (for example, of some of the large-scale social experiments for social policy). Consideration of these broader issues leads on to an examination of the political role of social science research and its place in the society in which it is carried out.

There is no agreed theory of research ethics with which to evaluate the merits of undertaking particular pieces of research. It is difficult to determine whether, and if so to what extent, research subjects may be harmed by particular research practices. One widespread approach is in terms of a utilitarian risk/benefit calculus, but this leaves several issues unresolved. Both risks and benefits are difficult to predict and to measure, harm to the individual can only with difficulty be weighted against societal benefits, and the investigator is usually the judge in his own case. Another approach is in terms of situational ethics, where the investigator weighs up the morally appropriate course of action in the actual research context. A different approach is in terms of absolute moral principles to be followed in all situations. No approach receives universal approval, and ethical decision making in research remains ultimately a matter of individual judgement as well as professional controversy.

One practical consequence both of the societal impact of research and the indeterminacy of ethical decision making about research has been a move toward greater regulation. Many professional associations of social scientists have their own ethical codes, to which members are expected to adhere. Various forms of peer review by a researcher's own department or institution are a more rigorous and direct form of oversight. The Institutional Review Boards now established by universities in the United States are one example of efforts to prevent unethical behaviour by social researchers.

Martin Bulmer
London School of Economics and Political Science

Further Reading

Barnes, J. A. (1980), *Who Should Know What? Social Science, Privacy and Ethics*, Cambridge.

Beauchamp, T. L. *et al.* (eds) (1982), *Ethical Issues in Social Science Research*, Baltimore.

Ethnographic Fieldwork

The modern field researcher has the double task of collecting data and analysing it. He must first describe events and customs from within, in order to search for patterns and to explore the cognitive maps of his subjects. This is ethnography. He has also to trace developments over time and to compare his findings with data in other societies. He must then provide insights into the factors influencing similarities, differences and developments. Basic to his task, however, is the quality of his own field data. His primary research method is participant observation, supplemented by a growing arsenal of research instruments.

Participant observation basically involves living for an extended period alongside the people being studied. This period can vary from several months to more than a year, depending among other things on the research problem and available funds. (In Eastern Europe short research expeditions are more common.) To get to know the people he is studying the ethnographer must as far as possible share their experiences. It is obviously essential for him to learn the local language.

Participant observation in a foreign culture is a deeply emotional, sometimes even a traumatic, experience. The hardships of fieldwork can be extreme, but so can the rewards. For months the ethnographer lives in close contact with his subjects. He shares pleasures and griefs, hardships and victories. He often becomes involved in their personal and group conflicts. He also has to face and solve the myriad problems of daily life in new strange surroundings, to learn to give new content to such familiar roles as friend, neighbour, husband and father, and to act these out in public under the critical eyes of his new neighbours. He must always be fair, pleasant and, above all, constantly available. He will be subject to pressure to take sides in personal disputes between close informants, to express openly his preference for a particular faction, political party or class. Unless his introduction into the community has been carefully prepared through high-status persons, he may have a marginal position. He then becomes fair game for other marginals in the community who seek him out. Since he is eager for friendship and contact, he reciprocates these advances and may thus become identified with the community's eccentrics and outcasts, thereby jeopardizing his own status and credibility. The pressure of new roles, experiences and conflicts can become intense. Energy and time are usually also in short supply. The ethnographer must spend up to a third of his time writing up his data.

Fieldwork is often a lonely experience. The fieldworker's own family, if they are with him, can provide warmth and companionship. It is a little island to which the researcher can withdraw to regain a measure of objectivity and distance from neighbours and informants. For a male, his family may be the only way he can gain some access to the world of women. Nonetheless, many fieldwork locations are unhealthy and dangerous. Has an ethnographer the right to expose members of his family to such risks in order to enhance his scientific effectiveness and/or to meet his own need for affection and comfort? Many ethnographers have taken such risks and have profited by them, while others have suffered.

The ethnographer often faces other moral dilemmas. In the field the first is how to explain his presence. If he is researching a sensitive subject, he may be obliged to use a cover story that 'stretches' the truth somewhat. For example, in the early 1960s I carried out research in Sicily into the failure of a community development project. In the process I hoped to achieve an understanding of Mafia activities. Because the project itself was highly controversial and because it is unhealthy in Sicily to advertise an interest in Mafia, I told people I was studying the impact of emigration, a critical issue at the time. People were very helpful, but their enthusiasm for the subject constrained me since they did not take seriously my interest in community development and Mafia. The ethnographer, if he can, should thus avoid 'cover stories'. But if he must adopt one, he should stick as close to the truth as he can. Still, operating under a cover he is not being honest and is deceiving people who have given him their trust.

Informants become friends. This creates another dilemma, for it leads to a very instrumental, and often dishonest, approach to friendship. The interest of science demands that you milk your informants. You do this by making them your friends, by exchanging confidences, giving presents, talking for hours about subjects which bore you. Are these friends or scientific objects? The subjects themselves often realize that they are being used. For some fieldworkers the scientific ends justify the means. They have no moral problem. For many others, however, the dilemma remains.

By no means all informants are friends. Many are crude manipulators, unpleasant at best and uncompromisingly untrustworthy. Some informants, even those the researcher regards as friends, may steal, cheat and lie. They may ridicule him in public in a way he does not fully comprehend, in order to enhance their own status.

Later an ethnographer will be faced with publishing data essential to his analysis which, if published, could damage persons who befriended him and trusted him with their confidences. To delete or alter events does violence to science; to publish is a betrayal of trust and may, in an extreme case, lead to injury, imprisonment or death. This is a moral problem which many ethnographers have had to face. The solutions range from 'publish and be damned' to production of fiction.

Participant observation is thus a many-sided research instrument. While it is the anthropologist's primary research tool, his toolbag is more extensive. Most anthropologists also spend much of their time analysing archives, taking village censuses and holding surveys. They may carry out comparative research in other communities. They ask informants not only to submit to formal interviews, but occasionally also to a battery of tests, to write down their own experiences and attitudes and to categorize animate and inanimate objects, including their kin and neighbours, the supernatural beings they worship and the vegetables they eat.

All ethnographers are obliged to spend a great deal of time writing up their diaries, notebooks, interviews. The consolidation, classification and filing of the volume of data is essential. It has been demonstrated that unless information gleaned from informants is written up immediately, it is soon forgotten.

In general male and female fieldworkers have similar experiences. However, some problems they face are specific to their gender. It is very difficult for a male ethnographer to obtain intimate information from female informants, or even to observe their daily life. On the other hand, women researchers often encounter difficulties if they pursue their investigation in such typical male reserves as the South European coffee bars and cafes. Although they encounter problems and barriers, female ethnographers are able to operate among men far more successfully than male researchers can among women.

Ethnographic fieldwork is challenging, fascinating and hard work. For many it is an emotional experience of the same order as a psychoanalytical encounter. But the task is not finished when the researcher returns from the field. Fieldwork is but a first step. His task ends only when he has completed the much more difficult and time-consuming chore of digesting his material, analysing it and presenting it in a readable and convincing form to his readers.

Jeremy Boissevain
University of Amsterdam

Further Reading

Boissevain, J. (1970), 'Fieldwork in Malta', in G. D. Spindler (ed.), *Being an Anthropologist: Fieldwork in Eleven Cultures*, New York.

Epstein, A. L. (ed.) (1967), *The Craft of Social Anthropology*, London.

Golde, P. (ed.) (1970), *Women in the Field: Anthropological Experiences*, Chicago.

Pelto, P. J. (1970), *Anthropological Research. The Structure of Inquiry*, New York.

Spradley, J. P. (1980), *Participant Observation*, New York.

See also: *ethics in social research; interviews and interviewing.*

Experimental Design

The Function of Experimental Design

Experiments involve introducing a planned intervention (usually referred to as a 'treatment') into a situation, in order to associate the treatment with resulting change. Experimental design facilitates this process in several ways:

(1) It translates all aspects of one's hypothesis – the statement of expected relation of changes to the intervention – into operational terms: subjects, behaviours, situation, equipment, procedures, and so on. These permit the hypothesis to be tested empirically.

(2) It rules out those alternative explanations which provide the most serious challenge to the treatment as *the* explanation for the change.

(3) It facilitates relating the changes to other variables, thus permitting better understanding of the relationship.

The Logic of Experimental Design

(1) The first step in experimental design is to translate expectations expressed in one's hypothesis into operational terms. The accuracy of this translation is critical. Misleading conclusions are likely to result from a treatment that inadequately represents that intended, or an insufficiently sensitive measure of change.

(2) Following stage 1, one must create a situation in which changes can be sensed. Sometimes one compares the pre- with the post-intervention condition of the experimental subjects. In other instances, experimental subjects may be compared with an untreated comparable group, a 'control group'. In still other instances, post-treatment condition is compared with estimates of the untreated state, for instance, test norms or regression estimates made from previous data or comparable groups.

(3) One then rules out whatever alternative explanations may be important rivals to that intended. For example, if a control group is used, the groups may not have been equivalent to begin with, or drop outs may make them non-equivalent at the end. Alternative explanations common to many studies have been identified (see below) but some may be unique to a study. For example, if subjects are allowed to complete a test at home,

their score may reflect more their ability to seek help than their own achievement.

(4) Assuming the data support one's expectations, these steps in the logic follow:

(a) since the results were as predicted;

(b) and since there is no reasonable explanation for the phenomenon other than the treatment (others having been ruled out by one's design);

(c) then the hypothesis escaped disconfirmation. While one cannot test the hypothesis in every situation, one infers from this one that similar predictions would prove accurate in like instances. With each such confirmation, confidence in the hypothesis increases, but a single disconfirmation, without a reasonable explanation, is sufficient to disprove it.

Experimental Control

It is difficult to provide sufficient experimental control to protect against every possible alternative explanation. Further, one typically buys protection at a price. For example, a laboratory gives more complete control, but laboratory circumstances are rarely like those to which one hopes to generalize. Yet, natural circumstances may provide too little control. Zimbardo, Anderson and Kabat (1981) supply an interesting example of this dilemma and its solution. They hypothesized that the paranoid behaviour frequent in elderly people was due to the gradual unnoticed loss of hearing common in old age. An expensive longitudinal design following subjects over time would have been inconclusive because of the subjects' varying social experiences. In addition, it would involve the ethical problem of withholding hearing loss information to see if paranoid behaviour developed.

The researchers devised a creative experimental design. Post-hypnotic suggestion produced a temporary unnoticed hearing loss in college student volunteers with resulting increase in paranoid behaviour. To eliminate rival alternative explanations, two control groups of similar subjects were established: one received post-hypnotic suggestion of a hearing loss of which they would be *aware* and another a neutral post-hypnotic suggestion in order to show that the hypnotic process itself did not induce paranoid behaviour. The paranoia was shown to follow only unnoticed induced hearing loss, and all subjects were exposed to controlled similar social experiences following the loss. Altogether, this is a clever use of experimental design for an otherwise difficult problem.

But using a laboratory-like setting is not without costs. Impressed by the scientific laboratory, subjects may have tried to please the researcher; here, the researchers, knowing which was the experimental group, may have unintentionally cued subjects to appropriate behaviour (Rosenthal, 1976). The verisimilitude of the hypnotically induced hearing loss to that which occurs in older people may be questioned, as may the use of college students.

Nearly every design choice involves trade-offs in the use of resources which might have been used to control something else. Part of the 'art' of design is finding a suitable middle ground, one realistic enough to generalize but permitting sufficient control.

The Criteria of Good Design

A good design reduces one's uncertainty that the variables are linked with some generally as hypothesized. Showing they are linked requires a combination of internal, statistical conclusion and construct validity as defined by Cook and Campbell (1979). Internal validity assures that variables are linked in the form in which they were manipulated or measured. Statistical conclusion validity assures appropriate use and interpretation of statistics. Construct validity assures that the form in which the variables were manipulated or measured is that hypothesized.

Similarly, demonstrating generality requires a combination of external and construct validity. External validity assures the applicability of the results to other persons, places and times; construct validity, to other ways of operationalizing the variables.

Good designs accomplish the above with the best use of all available resources, time and energy. They fit an appropriate formulation of the problem rather than one cut to fit design requirements. They accurately anticipate those alternative explanations most reasonable to one's audience. Finally, ethical standards and institutional and social constraints are observed – altogether, a complex but manageable set of criteria.

Common Alternative Explanations

Some common conditions provide as plausible explanations as the treatment. Called 'threats to validity', they have been most recently redefined by Cook and Campbell (1979). A sampling of these includes:

(1) *Testing* – Pre-treatment testing may affect post-treatment's, especially if the same test is used. A control group provides protection since its post-test would be equally affected.
(2) *Selection* – Those selected for the experimental group differ from their controls, for example, when the experimental group consists of all volunteers and the control group comprises the remainder. Remedy? Use only volunteers randomly assigned to experimental and control groups.
(3) *Testing by treatment interaction* – Subjects sensitized to aspects of a treatment by pre-testing react differently on post-testing. A post-test only design provides protection.

Common Designs

(1) *Single group designs* – These are often called time series designs; relations are inferred from the pattern of treatment and response over time:

   (a) For static situations: pre-measure, treat, post-measure.
   (b) For situations with a regular pattern: observe it, treat, and determine if the pattern is disturbed.
   (c) With either an irregular pattern or for an especially conclusive demonstration, relate the pattern of change to that of treatment, intentionally varying the latter's timing, length, strength and such factors.

Also referred to as AB, ABA, or ABABA designs (A is the untreated condition, B the treated), ABA and more complex designs are useful only where the change under the 'B' condition is impermanent. (For information on such designs see Kratochwill, 1978.)

(2) *Multiple group designs* – These designs may involve both multiple experimental and control groups (Zimbardo used two control groups). Groups are unlike as far as possible except for the conditions to which change is to be attributed. But, only one condition can be different between groups being compared. Assuring group equivalency is usually achieved by randomly assigning subjects. *On the average* this will equate them for everything, from length of eyelashes to motivation.

The simplest, yet a very effective, design involves post-testing only. Let 'R' indicate random assignment of subjects to groups, 'O' a test or observation, and 'X' treatment. Then it is diagrammed as:

$$R \qquad X \qquad O$$
$$R \qquad \qquad O$$

To assure that the groups were equivalent at the outset, a pretest may be added:

$$R \qquad O \qquad X \qquad O$$
$$R \qquad O \qquad \qquad O$$

But this introduces both testing and testing by treatment interaction as alternative explanations. For better control, the Solomon four group design combines the previous two:

$$R \qquad \qquad X \qquad O$$
$$R \qquad \qquad \qquad O$$
$$R \qquad O \qquad X \qquad O$$
$$R \qquad O \qquad \qquad O$$

Designs in which groups are not created by random assignment of subjects (same designs as above without the 'R') are designated quasi-experimental designs. Their strengths and weaknesses are explored in Campbell and Stanley (1963) and in Cook and Campbell (1979).

Blocking equates groups by the individual's random assignment from within a relatively homogeneous 'block'. Blocks are created by subdividing subjects into levels on a characteristic such as intelligence where non-equivalence is a serious threat to design validity. The matched pairs design is an extreme form of blocking.

(3) *Factorial designs* – Factorial designs permit analysis of the simultaneous effects of two or more treatments or related variables by providing a group for each possible combination. For instance, to study the effect on speed of prose memorization of (a) no emphasis, (b) italics and (c) underlining of important parts, and of printing them in (1) black or (2) red would require six groups – a 2×3 factorial design:

	No emphasis	Italics	Underlining
Black type			
Red type			

From this design one could learn which emphasis treatment or colour was best alone, and, if these factors interact, what combination of emphasis and colour is best. The latter is called an interaction effect. If a pre-test were given this would be a 'repeated measures 2×3 factorial design'.

(4) *Other designs* – As may be anticipated, the variety of designs is limited mainly by one's ingenuity. A number of designs have been borrowed from agriculture, such as the Latin and Graeco-Latin square and the split plot designs. These and others are described in Bow *et al.* (1978), Cochran and Cox (1957), Fisher (1966), Kirk (1982), and Winer (1971).

David R. Krathwohl
Syracuse University

References
Bow, G. E. P., Hunter, W. G. and Hunter, J. S. (1978), *Statistics for Experimenters: An Introduction to Design, Data Analysis and Model Building*, New York.
Campbell, D. T. and Stanley, J. C. (1963), 'Experimental and

quasi-experimental designs for research on teaching', in N. L. Gage (ed.), *Handbook of Research on Teaching*, Chicago.

Cochran, W. G. and Cox, G. M. (1957), *Experimental Design*, 2nd edn, New York.

Cook, T. D. and Campbell, D. T. (1979), *Quasi-Experimentation*, Chicago.

Fisher, R. A. (1966), *Design of Experiments*, 8th edn, New York.

Kirk, R. (1982), *Experimental Design*, 2nd edn, Belmont, Calif.

Kratochwill, T. R. (1978), *Single Subject Research: Strategies for Evaluation Change*, New York.

Rosenthal, R. (1976), *Experimenter Effects in Behavioural Research*, New York.

Winer, B. S. (1971), *Statistical Principles in Experimental Design*, 2nd edn, New York.

Zimbardo, P. G., Anderson, S. M. and Kabat, L. G. (1981), 'Induced hearing deficit generates experimental paranoia', *Science*, 212.

Feyerabend, Paul K. (1924–)

Paul K. Feyerabend, a leading philosopher of science, has fundamentally challenged the logical positivist account of the scientific method and, in addition, advocated an anarchistic theory of knowledge, relying on the works of such political theorists as J. S. Mill, Marx, Lenin and Trotsky. He emphasizes the significance of political action, propaganda and political thought for the study and practice of science.

Born in Vienna, Feyerabend was induced into the Austrian army during the Nazi occupation and at the end of World War II he read history, physics and astronomy at the University of Vienna. He received his doctorate in 1951 and then went to England to study with fellow Austrian philosopher, Ludwig Wittgenstein. But Wittgenstein's untimely death resulted in Feyerabend studying with the philosopher of science, Karl Popper – whose ideas about the nature and significance of science Feyerabend has been criticizing for many years. For the past 25 years he has taught at the University of California at Berkeley, and during this time has held several teaching positions at European universities as well.

Following numerous philosophical articles on the nature of

scientific inquiry, Feyerabend published in 1975 his well-known and provocative volume, *Against Method: Outline of an Anarchistic Theory of Knowledge*, which contains his vehement attack on the mainstream rationalist theory of scientific methodology. Feyerabend's thought becomes most relevant to social scientists in his conception of the traditional philosophical fields of logic, epistemology, and the philosophy of science as empirical inquiries requiring historical, sociological, psychological, anthropological and political data.

Some of Feyerabend's characteristic positions include his passionate rejection and fear of the stultifying consequences of one method of doing science which demands conformity on the part of scientists: 'Science is an essentially anarchistic enterprise: theoretical anarchism is more humanitarian and more likely to encourage progress than its law-and-order alternatives' (*Against Method*); and his corresponding deep commitment to fostering the conditions of maximum scientific creativity even to the point of claiming the creative value of violence! 'Violence . . . is *beneficial* for the individual, for it releases one's energies and makes one realize the powers at one's disposal' (*Against Method*). His admonition not to stifle scientists' creativity because of a dominant methodology is reflected in his renowned methodological credo for science of 'Anything Goes': 'All methodologies have their limitations and the only "rule" that survives is "anything goes" ' (*Against Method*).

Feyerabend argues for the democratic control of science by the lay public and replies to the critics of *Against Method* in his *Science in a Free Society* published in 1978.

Joel Kassiola
Brooklyn College of the City University of New York
See also: *Popper*.

Functional Analysis

The terms functional analysis and functionalism are often equated, yet to equate them is to beg a number of questions, is misleading and perhaps even mistaken.

Functionalism is a doctrine which asserts that the principal task of sociology and social anthropology is to examine the contribution which social items make to the social and cultural life of human collectivities; it may additionally assert that to examine social phenomena in this way is to explain why those items occur at all, and/or why they have persisted.

Functional analysis is a method of sociological or anthropological enquiry which consists in examining social and cultural items by locating them in a wider context. This usually means showing how these items affect and are affected by others with which they coexist over time.

From these descriptions it is clear why the doctrine is named functionalism: it claims that cultural phenomena either have uses, and otherwise would not endure, or that they come into being, and then persist, because they are useful. But it is not initially clear why a method of examining cultural phenomena within the context of other such items should be called functional, in the sense of 'useful'. The most obvious reason is that functional analysis has been seen as so necessary to functionalism that the two have been treated almost as one. To explain the function(s) of a social item does itself require locating it within the context of a wider system or subsystem. For example, in order to show that the function of kinship terminology is to express the shared recognition of a set of kinship categories, which are necessary to sustain rules of co-operation, alliance, marital eligibility, succession, inheritance, and so on, one has to examine kinship terms of reference and address in the contexts of rules governing different degrees and directions of kinship interaction. So much is obvious. What is not at all obvious is that the practice of functional analysis also presupposes that the doctrine of functionalism is true: in short, from the decision to locate the use of kinship terminology within the context of its various uses, it does not follow that that terminology owes its existence to those uses; it might be equally plausible to argue that the usages are consequent upon linguistic rules.

Here we encounter a second article of faith endorsed, unquestioningly in some cases, by earlier functionalist anthropologists: that, in the absence of written histories, or other reliable clues to the past, one must assume that some features of the here-and-now must be taken as given and as accounting for others;

and that both sets of features are readily identifiable. For example, it would be assumed that the level of technology, the system of ordering economic and political relations through kinship, and the form of that kinship system could be taken as given, and that certain other practices, such as linguistic and ritual norms (symbolic representations), could be explained as functioning to maintain those given features of social and cultural life.

Furthermore, it seems also to have been assumed that the effectiveness of the method of functional analysis attested to the strength of the theory, and that the theory justified the method.

Whether or not the theory could have justified the method, what did justify it were two sets of circumstances in which ethnographers of preliterate societies worked: (1) They dealt with societies with no written records and, it was often believed, with no other clear evidence which could illuminate the past and, consequently, the processes whereby the societies' existing features could have developed. Thus it seemed that all that ethnographers could do well was to examine certain existing practices and beliefs in their context, so as to make sense of them in comparison with the practices and beliefs of the societies in which ethnographic reports would be read. (2) They dealt with societies which, unlike their own, were relatively simple and slow-changing and, therefore, in which there appeared to be a high degree of interdependence of the different features of social and cultural life (Cohen, 1968).

To qualify the first point: the absence of evidence for recounting reliable histories of certain societies had not inhibited the anthropological precursors of functionalism from constructing histories that were informed either by the theory of evolutionary parallelism or by that of diffusionism. Functionalism and functional analysis emerged in reaction to these so-called histories. And, given the reaction against these seemingly unstable theories of pseudo-history and, moreover, their distracting effect on the examination of the here-and-now, it is likely that the commitment to functionalist doctrine was regarded not only as a necessary justification of the method, but as a rationalized refutation of the two doctrines of 'conjectural' history.

To qualify the second point, it should not be thought that

functionalists explicitly acknowledged the greater interdependence of different features of social life to be found in the technologically simpler and smaller-scale societies. Rather, it can be said that the significant degree of functional autonomy possessed by different features of social life in most complex societies is expressed in a language which treats different areas of social and cultural activity as separable, even when they are not altogether separate. This language, fashioned not for self-conscious social scientific discourse, but, rather, for everyday use, was imposed on societies within which such categories were for the most part foreign. Thus, certain activities were separated out by the use of the ethnographers' taken-for-granted language and then shown to be more or less strongly interrelated. But few, if any, such ethnographers recognized that the degree of interconnectedness which constitutes a social and cultural system might itself vary from one such system to another. Moreover, some interpretations of the method encouraged an undue emphasis on the degree and nature of the interconnectedness of social and cultural phenomena in even the simplest societies, and, also, promoted an even greater error in the excessive search for it in more complex societies.

The almost casual equation of method and doctrine by some social anthropologists was highly misleading: the doctrine that functional analysis could also yield explanations of the existence of social and cultural phenomena was in many instances not even demonstrated and was, in any case, at worst erroneous and at best confusing.

But what use of functional analysis of the here-and-now has ever explained why the Bemba are matrilineal, why the Tallensi have no centralized political authority, why the Nuer have a form of monotheism, or why some Australian aboriginal societies have moeities and others, in almost the same physical environment, do not? While a functional analysis of Nuer feuds might be thought to account for their forms by showing how these forms serve to maintain particular patterns of kin-based alignments, it could hardly account for the segmentary structure of that society. Of course, if one knows that the Nuer have a particular type of segmentary structure, characterized by particular processes of alignment and division, that knowledge might help explain why, if certain other conditions remain constant, that structure tends to perpetuate and to resist transformation into a more centralized type of society. Such an explanation of social reproduction – which could be called an equilibrium analysis, since it shows that the processes which inhere in this type of structure are self-correcting with regard to the non-centralization of power – does not itself rest on any part of the functionalist doctrine.

As philosophical critics, followed in turn by social scientists, have long shown, those explanations of social phenomena which are truly and simply functionalist are seriously flawed: they are teleological in that they account for items by examining their positive consequences in maintaining a wider system of which they are a part; and they reify such systems by treating them as though they were either mechanical or organic wholes (Nagel, 1956).

The only reply to such critics is to argue that functional analysis may demonstrate a continuous, circular flow of causes and effects – that is, of so-called feedback processes – which show how a system persists, and therefore explains why particular items are to be found at a particular time and place. But even if this can be done convincingly – and it requires empirical confirmation, not simply an intuitive judgement that coexisting phenomena must interrelate in this self-maintaining way – it hardly attests to the value of a functionalist doctrine. Rather, it illustrates the point that social and cultural persistence may in some cases be explained in terms of 'systemic feedback' or, if one prefers, in terms of benign chains of cause and effect which are at some points recursive.

But, of course, the outcome of such causal chains may not be benign, at least to some sections of a society. For example, the educational systems of (most) industrial societies favour the children of the advantaged, whose environments not only facilitate educational performance but may also strengthen and channel motivation to succeed in it. But, since structured inequalities of performance contradict the principle of equality of opportunity, it could be argued that while the system 'functions' for the advantaged it does not do so for the disadvantaged and, especially, not where the latter are aware of the discrepancy between principle and reality. However, ardent functionalists might show that the system works effectively at creating only a low level of motivation among those who are least likely to succeed and, thus, in this way *does* function to maintain both itself and a degree of wider social stability. On the other hand, it could be said that the symbols of alienation with which the disadvantaged young adorn themselves signify an ill-contained and, perhaps, ill-defined discontent which they occasionally express in more overt fashion. But then one could also argue that those expressive symbols also serve the wider system; and so on (Merton, 1949).

But what of those situations in which the working of the system benefits no one? In some circumstances of low, or even zero, economic growth, the institutionalized forms of conflict over income levels and differentials could become so intensified as to contribute to a negative growth rate and to an uneven but overall fall in real incomes. One could argue even here that the seeming dysfunctions of the systems are, after all, functional for it: since the contending parties cannot unite to change a system which no one wants in its existing form, their inactions contribute to its persistence.

What such an example demonstrates is that the term functional, meaning 'useful', pertains only to those circumstances in which the gratification of the conscious or unconscious motives of social actors is (intentionally or unintentionally) facilitated by certain enduring practices, which sustain those motives, and which in turn contribute to the continuation of the practices themselves. No other use of the term can be permitted. Certainly, to refer to social practices as functioning to maintain a system, regardless of whether any groups or collectivities have an interest in maintaining it, is either to state the obvious – that a system persists – or it is to beg the very question that needs to be answered. And if the answer is negative, then either the use of the term function creates a self-contradiction or it is meretriciously redundant.

What has been called functional analysis should, in fact, be seen as a particular form of the systems approach in the social sciences. To state that there is a system is to imply that discernibly separable processes interact so as to endure in this state over a period of time. To enquire as to why particular features of that system persist is to locate those features in the wider system. To establish that some social practice, which is part of a system, gratifies the motives of some social members, is to ascribe a function to that practice.

Percy S. Cohen
London School of Economics and Political Science

References
Cohen, P. S. (1968), *Modern Social Theory*, London.
Merton, R. K. (1949), 'Manifest and latent functions', in *Social Theory and Social Structure*, Glencoe, Ill.
Nagel, E. (1956), 'A formalization of functionalism', in *Logic Without Metaphysics*, Glencoe, Ill.

Further Reading
Davis, K. (1959), 'The myth of functional analysis as a special method in sociology and anthropology', *American Sociological Review*, 24.

Game Theory

The theory of games is a branch of mathematics devoted to the study of interdependent decision making. It applies to any social situation in which: (1) there are two or more decision makers, called *players*, each with a choice of two or more courses of action, called *strategies*; (2) the outcome depends on the strategy choices of all the players; and (3) each player has well-defined preferences among the possible outcomes, so that numerical payoffs reflecting these preferences can be assigned. Games such as chess and poker, together with many social, economic, political and military conflicts which are not commonly thought of as games, possess these properties and are therefore amenable in principle to game theory analysis. The primary goal of the theory is to determine, through formal reasoning alone, what strategies the players ought to choose in order to pursue their interests rationally, and what outcomes will result if they do so.

Although some progress was made by Zermelo in 1912, and by Borel during the early 1920s, the theory was not firmly established until John von Neumann proved the fundamental minimax theorem in 1928. This theorem applies to two-person, strictly competitive (zero-sum) games, in which one player's payoffs are simply the negatives of the other player's. If the number of strategies is finite, and the players are permitted to use randomizing devices to 'choose' weighted averages of their strategies, then each player can adopt a strategy that yields the best payoff given the most damaging counter-strategies available to the adversary. The minimax theorem asserts that these payoffs are equal, and that every game of this type therefore has a well-defined solution.

Applications of game theory in the social sciences have focused chiefly on non-zero-sum games. A famous example is the two-person *Prisoner's Dilemma*, identified in 1951 by Merrill Flood and later explicitly formulated and named by Albert W. Tucker. This game has the paradoxical property that whereas each player has a *dominant* strategy that yields the best payoff against both of the opponent's available counter-strategies, each player obtains a better payoff if both choose *dominated* strategies. A multi-person generalization of this, the *N-Person Prisoner's Dilemma*, was discovered in the early 1970s; in this game, every player is better off if all choose dominated strategies than if all choose dominant strategies. The N-Person Prisoner's Dilemma is a model of many familiar social problems, including resource conservation, wage inflation, environmental pollution, and arms races.

Experimental games have been used by psychologists to study co-operation and competition in two-person and multi-person groups, and economists have applied game theory to the study of bargaining and collective choice. In political science and sociology, game theory has been used to analyse voting behaviour and coalition formation, and numerous other applications of the theory in social anthropology and other fields have been attempted. During the 1970s, applications of the theory to the study of the evolution of social behaviour began to flourish in sociobiology.

Andrew M. Colman
University of Leicester

Further Reading
Colman, A. M. (1982), *Game Theory and Experimental Games: The Study of Strategic Interaction*, Oxford.
Von Neumann, J. and Morgenstern, O. (1953), *Theory of Games and Economic Behavior*, 3rd edn, Princeton.
See also: *game theory, economic applications*.

Game Theory, Economic Applications

The popularity of game theory has varied considerably since its introduction into economics by J. von Neumann and O. Morgenstern in their 1944 classic *The Theory of Games and Economic Behavior*. Game theory is an attempt to analyse rational strategic behaviour in situations of uncertainty. The initial applications of the theory were to oligopoly theory, and in the 1950s this strand of development seemed to come to an end. After a lull game theory was applied to general equilibrium theory and has given some fruitful insights into the structure of competitive equilibria through concepts such as 'the core'. Game theorists were able to show that competitive equilibrium was only possible if rational agents could not form blocking coalitions to improve their own position at the expense of the non-coalition actors in the situation. Recently there has been a new wave of interest in game theory. This has had three dimensions, all associated with attempts to analyse economic and social institutions. The three areas are: (1) the analysis of markets and monetary institutions; (2) the analysis of planning processes; and (3) in the area of social choice and welfare economics. Game theory has been used for both analytical and normative problems in all these areas.

One major advance has been the introduction of the concept of incentive compatibility as a constraint on action. The idea is simple: any agent, when designing his strategy, should take account of the fact that the other players will only act in their own best interests. If a player wants others to act, then he should only undertake actions that give others incentives to comply. This analytical concept has been extremely useful in aiding our understanding of bargaining and contracting in labour markets in franchising contracts, and in the analysis of the impact of taxes. It is not so much a new behavioural concept as a recognition of the obvious constraints a rational actor will face. A related set of ideas has been used in the public-choice literature where researchers have been trying to design games where individuals will reveal their true preferences. These ideas have been particularly useful in looking at feasible public utility pricing schemes and in looking at the properties of voting schemes.

Some recent developments in the theory of games have aided our understanding of the market process. The concept of a game can be applied to a process that repeats itself over time. For instance the problem of oligopolistic pricing can be seen as a repeated game problem. Standard tools can be applied, and it has been discovered that if the length of the game is finite, then in the last period the analysis to apply is that of the one-period game. But if this is known in the period before last, then the same applies to the period before last (this is sometimes known as the chainstore paradox). If one period analysis applies, then the development of 'reputation' and 'reliability' are not possible. It is possible to analyse these concepts in the concept of an infinite (or never-ending) game, where reputation effects change solutions. These concepts have usefully been adopted in the analysis of monetary institutions, in the study of oligopoly, and, most recently, in the analysis of general economic equilibrium.

Often in game theory the results are much less impressive than the techniques used, and new concepts, such as discounted games, are often more useful for telling us where the blind alleys are rather than where they are not. Despite this, clear advances have recently been made in the application of game theory based on agents whose expectations are in some sense 'rational' (in perfect equilibrium games) and whose actions are incentive compatible. After several false starts game theory now appears to be an indispensable part of the economist's tool-kit. An excellent recent survey may be found in *The Journal of Economic Literature*, June 1981, by A. Schotter and G. Schwodjauer.

Ray Barrell
University of Southampton

General Systems Theory

General Systems Theory in the broadest sense refers to a collection of general concepts, principles, tools, problems and methods associated with systems of any kind. As such, it is not a theory in the usual sense, but rather a field of study. To avoid confusion, it is often referred to as General Systems Research.

The terms general system and general systems theory were first used by Ludwig von Bertalanffy in the early 1930s, although the first written presentations appeared only after the Second World War (von Bertalanffy, 1950).

Von Bertalanffy was not only the originator of general systems theory, but also one of the major organizers of the general systems movement, represented initially by the Society for General Systems Research (established in 1954, originally under the name 'Society for the Advancement of General Systems Theory'), and extended later to the other organizations and activities (Cavallo, 1979). The Society was founded with the following objectives:

(1) To investigate the isomorphy of concepts, laws and models from various fields, and to help in useful transfers from one field to another.
(2) To encourage development of adequate theoretical models in fields which lack them.
(3) To minimize the duplication of theoretical effort in different fields.
(4) To promote the unity of science through improving communication among specialists.

System is typically defined as 'a set or arrangement of things so related or connected as to form a unity or organic whole' (*Webster's New World Dictionary*). To follow this common definition, a system consists of a set of some things, say set T, and some sort of relation among the things, say relation R. That is, a system is an ordered pair S= (T,R), where S denotes a system. The term 'relation' is used here in a broad sense to encompass the whole set of kindred terms such as constraint, structure, information, organization, interaction, dependence, correlation, cohesion, coupling, linkage, interconnection, pattern, and the like.

The common-sense conception of systems as ordered pairs (T,R) is too general and, consequently, of little pragmatic value. To make it useful it must be refined in the sense that specific classes of the ordered pairs are introduced. Such classes can basically be introduced by (i) restricting set T to certain kind of things, or (ii) by restricting relation R to certain kind of relations.

Classification criteria (i) and (ii) are independent of each other. Criterion (i) is exemplified by the traditional classification of science and technology into disciplines and specializations, each focusing on the study of certain kinds of things (physical, chemical, biological, political, economical, etc.) without committing to any particular kind of relations. Criterion (ii) leads to fundamentally different classes of systems, each characterized by a specific kind of relation but not committed to any particular kind of things for which the relation is defined.

Since different kinds of things require different experimental (instrumentation) procedures for data acquisition, the classification of systems based on criterion (i) is essentially *experimentally based*. Criterion (ii), on the other hand, is primarily relevant to data processing of all kinds rather than data acquisition; as such, it is predominantly *theoretically based*.

The largest classes of systems based on criterion (ii) are those which characterize various *epistemological types of systems*, that is, types of knowledge regarding the phenomena under consideration. These types are naturally ordered. This ordering, which is often referred to as an *epistemological hierarchy of systems*, is vital to a comprehensive characterization of systems problems and the development of methodological tools to deal with them (Klir, 1979, 1985; Zeigler, 1974, 1976).

Each class of systems defined by a particular epistemological type is further refined by various *methodological distinctions*. Problems that are associated with systems characterized by the same epistemological type and methodological distinction can be handled by the same kind of methods. These classes of systems are further divided into still smaller classes. Each of these classes consists of systems that are equivalent with respect to *some* specific, pragmatically significant aspects of their relations.

The smallest classes of systems are reached when systems in each class are required to be equivalent in *all* aspects of their relations. Such equivalence is usually called *isomorphism* between systems, and classes based on it are called *isomorphic classes of systems*.

While systems in each isomorphic equivalence class are totally equivalent in their relations, they may be based on completely different kinds of things. To deal with relational aspects of systems, it is sufficient to replace each isomorphic class of systems by a single system as its representative. Although the choice of these representatives is arbitrary, in principle it is important that the same selection criteria be used for all isomorphic classes.

When systems representing the individual equivalence classes are required to be defined on some purely abstract (interpretation-free) entities and their relations are described in some convenient standard form (for example, in a specific mathematical or programming language), they are called *general systems*. Hence, a general system is a standard and interpretation-free system chosen to represent a class of systems equivalent (isomorphic) with respect to all relational aspects that are pragmatically relevant in a given context. *General systems theory* (or research) is the study of the full scope of relational phenomena conceptualized as various types (epistemological and methodological) of general systems.

George J. Klir
State University of New York, Binghamton

References

Bertalanffy, L. von (1950), 'An outline of general systems theory', *British Journal of the Philosophy of Science*, 1.

Cavallo, R. E. (ed.) (1979), 'Systems research movement: characteristics, accomplishments, and current developments', *General Systems Bulletin*, 9.

Klir, G. J. (1979), 'General systems problem solving methodology', in B. Zeigler *et al.* (eds), *Modelling and Simulation Methodology*, Amsterdam.

Klir, G. J. (1985), *Architecture of Systems Problem Solving*, New York.

Zeigler, B. P. (1974), *Theory of Modelling and Simulation*, New York.

Zeigler, B. P. (1976), 'The hierarchy of system specifications and the problem of structural inference', *PSA 1976*, East Lansing, Michigan.

Further Reading

Ashby, W. R. (1956), *An Introduction to Cybernetics*, New York.

Bertalanffy, L. von (1968), *General Systems Theory*, New York.

Cavallo, R. E. (1979), *The Role of Systems Methodology in Social Science Research*, New York.

Mesarovic, M. D. and Takahara, Y. (1975), *General Systems Theory: Mathematical Foundations*, New York.

See also: *mathematical models*.

Graph Theory

Graph theory (Harary, 1969) is a branch of topology and the cornerstone of combinatorics. It studies patterns of relationships among pairs of abstract elements. Represented pictorially, a graph consists of a point set with some points joined by lines (see Figure 1). Common empirical interpretations of graphs are social networks and genealogical trees where the points represent persons and the lines relations of communication and descent respectively. Leonhard Euler began the formal study of graph theory in 1736 when he resolved the celebrated Königsberg Bridge Problem. There have been numerous rediscoveries of graph theory since then. Thus, Cayley utilized tree-graphs to enumerate organic chemical isomers, and the physicist Kirchhoff initiated electrical engineering, modelling the topology of an electrical network by its abstract graph.

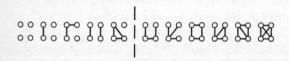

Figure 1: The graphs with four points

Firmly established in the natural sciences, graph theory has become the essential model for structural analysis in the social sciences. First explicitly applied in social psychology – for example, to the analysis of balance in cognitive structures, and status in organizations (Harary, Norman and Cartwright, 1965) – it was the natural model for social network studies concerning the effects of direct and indirect connections on individual and group behaviour (Barnes, 1972). The current multidisciplinary interest in graph theory in computer and social science is reflected in the new journal, *Social Networks*.

The expanding range of real world applications of graph theory is shown by recent results in anthropology (Hage and Harary, 1983) which draw on all adjacent disciplines. The distance between points in a graph is essential for studying the relative centrality of communities in trade networks and for articulating the interaction between mediated communication and power in informal political systems. A signed graph has positive and negative values on its lines; here the concepts of balance and clustering serve to explicate folk theories of consistency in kinship relations, and they model the evolution of political alliances. Directed graphs or digraphs (those with arrows on the lines) give highly intuitive representations of logical relations and thus facilitate the purely formal, comparative approach to social structure originally proposed by Lévi-Strauss. The concept of structural duality in graphs – dual operations applied to each type of graph, ordinary, signed and directed – yields transformation rules for myths and disentangles the variety of meanings of 'opposite' in structural analysis. The interactions between graphs and groups make explicit the permutational models evoked in structuralism. Finally, networks (graphs or digraphs with numerical values on the lines) enable the analysis of group processes such as fission and fusion. The probabilistic theory of Markov chains provides models for simulating subsistence practices where the ethnographic record is weak or absent.

The attractions of graph theory for the practising social scientist (whether anthropologist, archaeologist, economist, geographer, historian, political scientist, psychologist or sociologist) are fourfold: (1) The models are iconic and intuitively meaningful. (2) The language is rich as well as exact and thus is just as applicable to the analysis of efficacy in primitive mnemonics as connectivity in social networks. (3) There are techniques for the calculation of quantitative aspects of structure through the application of matrix algebra. (4) Finally, graph theory contains theorems which enable one to draw conclusions about certain properties of a structure from knowledge of other properties.

Per Hage
University of Utah

Frank Harary
University of Michigan

References
Barnes, J. A. (1972), *Social Networks*, Reading, Mass.
Hage, P. and Harary, F. (1983), *Structural Models in
    Anthropology*, Cambridge.
Harary, F. (1969), *Graph Theory*, Reading, Mass.
Harary, F., Norman, R. Z. and Cartwright, D. (1965),
    Structural Models: An Introduction To the Theory of Directed Graphs,
    New York.
See also: *networks*.

Habermas, Jürgen (1929–)

Jürgen Habermas has been the most prolific and influential representative of the 'second generation' of the Frankfurt School. He has both continued the theoretical tradition of his teachers Adorno and Horkheimer and his friend Marcuse, and has also significantly departed from 'classical' critical theory and made many important new contributions to contemporary philosophy and social theory. In particular, he has opened critical theory to a dialogue with other philosophies and social theories such as the hermeneutics of Gadamer, systems theory and structural functionalism, empirical social sciences, analytic and linguistic philosophy, and theories of cognitive and moral development. In recent years, he has been synthesizing these influences into a theory of 'communicative action', which presents the foundation and framework of a social theory that builds on the tradition of Marx, Weber and classical critical theory, but which also criticizes his predecessors and breaks new theoretical ground.

Habermas was born on 18 June 1929 in Dusseldorf, and grew up in Gummersbach, Germany. His father was head of the Bureau of Industry and Trade, and his grandfather was a minister and director of the local seminary. He experienced the rise and defeat of Fascism, and was politicized by the Nuremberg trials and documentary films of the concentration camps shown after the war. Habermas began his university studies in Göttingen in 1949 and finished a dissertation of *Das Absolute und die Geschichte* in 1954. In the 1950s, Habermas studied – and was strongly influenced by – Lukács's *History and Class Consciousness* and Adorno and Horkheimer's *Dialectic of Enlightenment* which he first read in 1955. He studied the young Marx and the young Hegelians with Karl Löwith, one of Germany's great scholars and teachers.

Habermas resolved to work with Adorno and Horkheimer because he believed that they were establishing a dialectical and critical theory of society from within a creative and innovative Marxist tradition. He thus went to Frankfurt and continued his studies in the Institute for Social Research. In this context, he wrote his first major book *Strukturwandel der Öffentlichkeit* (1962). Combining historical and empirical research with the theoretical framework of critical theory, Habermas traced the historical rise and decline of what he called the 'bourgeois public sphere' and its replacement by the mass media, technocratic administration, and societal depoliticization. This influential work continues to animate discussion concerning problems of representative democracy in contemporary capitalist societies and the need for more participatory, democratic and egalitarian spheres of sociopolitical discussion and debate.

In the 1960s, Habermas taught at the Universities of Heidelberg (from 1961–4) and Frankfurt (from 1964–71). At this time he also became more interested in politics and published *Student und Politik* with others in 1961 which called for university reforms, and *Protestbewegung und Hochschulreform* in 1969 which continued his concern with university reform and also criticized what he saw as the excesses of the German student movement in the 1960s. Habermas was also engaged in intense theoretical work during this period. His *Theorie und Praxis* appeared in 1963 (*Theory and Practice*, Boston, 1973), which contained theoretical papers on major classical and contemporary social and political theorists, as well as anticipations of his own theoretical position; *Zur Logik der Sozialwissenschaften* in 1967 contained a detailed and critical summary of contemporary debates in the logic of the social sciences; *Erkenntnis und Interesse* in 1968 (*Knowledge and Human Interests*, Boston, 1971) traced the development of epistemology and critical social theory from Kant to the present; and several collections of essays: *Technik und Wissenschaft als Ideologie* (1968); *Arbeit-Erkenntnis-Fortschritt* (1970); and *Philosophische-politische Profile* (1971).

During the 1970s Habermas intensified his studies of the social sciences and began restructuring critical theory as communication theory. Key stages of this enterprise are contained in a collection of studies written with Niklas Luhmann, *Theorie der Gesellschaft oder Sozialtechnologie* (1971); *Legitimationsprobleme im Spätkapitalismus* (1973); *Zur Rekonstruktion des Historischen Materialismus* (1976); and essays collected in several other books. In these works, Habermas sharpened his critique of classical Marxism and his critical theory predecessors. He attempted to develop his own reconstruction of historical materialism, a critical theory of society, and a philosophical theory rooted in analyses of communicative action. During much of this period since 1971, Habermas was director of the Max Planck Institute in Starnberg where he involved himself in various research projects and was in close touch with developments in the social sciences. After a series of disputes with students and colleagues, he resigned in 1982 and returned to Frankfurt where he is now Professor of Philosophy and Sociology.

In 1981, Habermas published his two-volume magnum opus, *Theorie des kommunikativen Handelns*. This impressive work of historical scholarship and theoretical construction appraises the legacies of Marx, Durkheim, Weber, Lukács and 'Western Marxism', including critical theory, and criticizes their tendencies towards theoretical reductionism and their failure to develop an adequate theory of communicative action and rationality. Habermas also contributes his own analysis of the importance of communicative action and rationality for contemporary social theory. The book points both to his continuity with the first generation of the Frankfurt school and his significant departures. *Theorie des kommunikativen Handelns* also manifests Habermas's continued interest in the relationship between theory and practice with his discussion of new social movements. The concluding section is a testament to his interest in systematic social theory with a practical intent in his summation of the status of critical theory today. The work as a whole thus sums up Habermas's last decade of theoretical work and points to some issues and topics that will probably constitute future projects. Habermas's legacy thus remains open to new theoretical and political developments and is an important part of contemporary discussions within social theory and science.

Douglas Kellner
University of Texas, Austin

Further Reading
Horster, D. and von Reijen, W. (1979), 'Interview with Jürgen Habermas', *New German Critique*, 18.
McCarthy, T. (1978), *The Critical Theory of Jürgen Habermas*, London.

Hermeneutics

Hermeneutics is a term used to describe the views of a variety of authors who have been concerned with problems of 'understanding' and 'interpretation'. Some of the themes of hermeneutics were introduced to English-speaking social scientists by the writings of Max Weber. As a participant in the methodological debates which occurred in Germany during the late nineteenth and early twentieth centuries, Weber was familiar with the views of philosophers and historians such as Wilhelm Dilthey, Heinrich Rickert and Wilhelm Windleband, who all argued that the study of the social and historical world requires the use of methods which are different from those employed in the investigation of natural phenomena. These arguments were reflected in Weber's own emphasis on the concept of under-standing or *verstehen*.

While Weber played an important role in introducing many social scientists to the ideas of hermeneutics, the latter tradition stretches back to a period well before Weber's time. Hermen-eutics derives from the Greek verb *hermēneuein*, which means to make something clear, to announce or to unveil a message. The discipline of hermeneutics first arose, one could say, with the interpretation of Homer and other poets during the age of the Greek Enlightenment. From then on, hermeneutics was closely linked to philology and textual criticism. It became a very important discipline during the Reformation, when Protestants challenged the right of tradition to determine the interpretation of the holy scriptures. Both classical scholars and theologians attempted to elaborate the rules and conditions which governed the valid interpretation of texts.

The scope of hermeneutics was greatly extended by Wilhelm Dilthey (in the nineteenth century). An historian as well as a philosopher, Dilthey was aware that texts were merely one form of what he called 'objectifications of life'. So the problem of interpretation had to be related to the more general question of how knowledge of the social-historical world is possible. Such knowledge is based, in Dilthey's view, on the interrelation of experience, expression and understanding. Cultural phenomena, such as texts, works of art, actions and gestures, are purposive expressions of human life. They are objectified in a sphere of conventions and values which are collectively shared, in the way that a person's attitude may be objectified in the medium of language. To understand cultural phenomena is to grasp them as objectified expressions of life; and ultimately it is to re-experience the creative act, to relive the experience of another. While reorienting hermeneutics towards a reflection on the foundations of the *Geisteswissenschaften* or 'human sciences', Dilthey's writings preserved a tension between the quest for objectivity and the legacy of Romanticism.

The key figure in twentieth-century hermeneutics is Martin Heidegger. Whereas in Dilthey's work the hermeneutical problem is linked to the question of *knowledge*, in Heidegger's it is tied to the question of *being*: problems of understanding and interpretation are encountered while unfolding the fundamental features of our 'being-in-the-world'. For Heidegger, 'understanding' is first and foremost a matter of projecting what we are capable of. This anticipatory character of understanding is a reformulation, in ontological terms, of what is commonly called the 'hermeneutical circle'. Just as we understand part of a text by anticipating the structure of the whole, so too all understanding involves a 'pre-understanding' which attests to the primordial unity of subject and object. We are beings-in-the-world, familiar with and caring for what is ready-to-hand, before we are subjects claiming to have knowledge *about* objects in the world.

Heidegger's work has implications for the way that the human sciences are conceived, as Hans-Georg Gadamer has attempted to show. In *Truth and Method* (1975), Gadamer establishes a connection between the anticipatory character of understanding and the interrelated notions of prejudice, authority and tradition. The assumption that prejudices are necessarily negative is itself an unjustified prejudice stemming, in Gadamer's view, from the Enlightenment. It is an assumption which has prevented us from seeing that understanding always requires pre-judgement or 'prejudice', that there are 'legitimate prejudices' based on the recognition of authority, and that one form of authority which has a particular value is tradition. We are always immersed in traditions which provide us with the prejudices that make understanding possible. Hence there can be no standpoint outside of history from which the totality of historical effects could be grasped; instead, understanding must be seen as an open and continuously renewed 'fusion' of historical 'horizons'.

Gadamer's provocative thesis was challenged in the mid-1960s by Jürgen Habermas and other representatives of 'critical theory'. While acknowledging the importance of Gadamer's hermeneutics for the philosophy of the human sciences, Habermas attacked the link between understanding and tradition. For such a link underplays the extent to which tradition may *also* be a source of power which distorts the process of communication and which calls for critical reflection. Appealing to the model of psychoanalysis, Habermas sketched the framework for a 'depth-hermeneutical' discipline which would be oriented to the idea of emancipation.

The debate between hermeneutics and critical theory has been reappraised by Paul Ricoeur. As a hermeneutic philosopher concerned with critique, Ricoeur has tried to mediate between the positions of Gadamer and Habermas by re-emphasizing the concept of the text. In contrast to the experience of belonging to a tradition, the text presupposes a distance or 'distanciation' from the social, historical and psychological conditions of its production. The interpretation of a text, involving both the structural explanation of its 'sense' and the creative projection of its 'reference', thus allows for the possibility of establishing a critical relation *vis-à-vis* 'the world' as well as 'the self'. Ricoeur shows how the model of the text and the method of text interpretation can be fruitfully extended to the study of such varied phenomena as metaphor, action and the unconscious.

As recent debates indicate, the issues which for centuries have been discussed under the rubric of hermeneutics are still very much alive. The appreciation of texts and works of art, the study of action and institutions, the philosophy of science and social science: in all of these spheres, problems of understanding and interpretation are recognized as central. While few contemporary hermeneutic philosophers would wish to draw the distinction between the natural sciences and the *Geisteswissenschaften* in the way that their nineteenth-century predecessors did, many would nevertheless want to defend the peculiar character of social and historical inquiry. For the *objects* of such inquiry are the product of *subjects* capable of action and understanding, so that our knowledge of the social and historical world cannot be sharply separated from the subjects who make up that world.

John B. Thompson
Jesus College, Cambridge

References

Gadamer, H.-G. (1975), *Truth and Method*, London. (Original German edn, *Wahrheit und Methode*, Tübingen, 1960.)

Palmer, R. E. (1969), *Hermeneutics: Interpretation Theory in Schleiermacher, Dilthey, Heidegger, and Gadamer*, Evanston, Ill.

Ricoeur, P, (1981), *Hermeneutics and the Human Sciences: Essays on Language, Action and Interpretation*, ed. and trans. J. B. Thompson, Cambridge.

See also: *Habermas*.

Index Numbers

Index numbers are constructed essentially as a way of representing a vector of variables by means of a single scalar variable. Clearly there is no uniquely correct way of accomplishing this transformation, and thus a considerable discussion on the implications of different approaches has developed. Economic statisticians have been particularly concerned with two types of scalar representation of vectors: (1) attempts have been made to represent changes in prices by a single price index, and (2) to reduce movements in quantities to a single quantity index, although of course on occasions one may want to reduce other variables to a simple scalar form.

Historically the problem of measuring price movements preceded the quantity analog. The former have always been a more sensitive issue. Early discussion on the subject tended to consider the price of just one commodity, often that of gold. A reduction in the gold content of coinage achieved through debasement of the currency was regarded as the same thing as an increase in the price level. In the last decade of the eighteenth century, the United Kingdom suspended the convertibility of paper money into gold. The subsequent debate on the inflation of prices was then focused on the price of gold bullion in terms of paper money.

The measurement of the price level with reference to one particular price may have been a useful way to determine the magnitude of a sudden marked debasement, and it is still used under circumstances where the value of currency is falling rapidly. (The tendency in Israel to fix prices in US dollars can be seen as an example of this.) However, it is scarcely satisfactory for comparisons over a longer period in which relative prices can change a great deal. It is in order to cope with this problem that the theory of price indices has been developed.

A price index attempts to compare the price level at one time with that of another period, or to compare relative prices in two different places. It is thus always measured relative to a base level (usually 100) and is not absolute in any sense. Early price indices relied on the simple sum of prices divided by the sum of prices in the base period $\Sigma p_t / \Sigma p_0$, or the simple arithmetic average of relative prices $1/n \Sigma (p_t / p_0)$ (p_t represents current prices and p_0 base prices). Neither of these is very satisfactory because some commodities are clearly more important than others. If one is trying to measure the change in price of national consumption, it is not very sensible to give the same importance to items which occupy only a small part in the consumption basket as to those which feature prominently. Although the idea of weighting so as to reflect relative importance can be traced back to the early nineteenth century, it is the mid-nineteenth century proposals of Laspeyres and Paasche which remain of great practical importance to the present day. Laspeyres suggested that one should observe the quantities bought in the base period, and derive the price index, I_t^L, as the ratio of their cost in the current period to that in the base period. $I_t^L = \Sigma p_t q_0 / \Sigma p_0 q_0$, where p_t, p_0 are as defined above and q_0 are base period quantities. Paasche proposed current rather than base period weights yielding the price index I_t^P as $I_t^P = \Sigma p_t q_t / \Sigma p_0 q_t$.

Most countries which publish consumer price indices adopt the Laspeyres index because, although the prices have to be measured on each occasion an index is calculated, the quantities used as weights only need to be calculated once, usually from an expenditure survey. In any case the time needed to process an expenditure survey means it is not possible to produce a timely Paasche price index. However it is clear that the weights used in a Laspeyres index can become stale. Expenditure will tend to shift towards goods which become relatively cheaper, and thus a Paasche price index will normally be lower than a Laspeyres index and the gap will tend to increase over time as the Laspeyres weights become increasingly outdated. This problem is usually resolved by updating the weights periodically. A link can be made by calculating indices for one period based on both old and new weights. The United Kingdom is perhaps unusual in updating the weights in its Retail Price

Index every year, based on the average consumption pattern in the three previous years. But even here the Laspeyres weights can be very unsuitable if, for example, a seasonal food becomes scarce, with a high price in one particular year.

Quantity indices are constructed in a similar fashion to price indices. When measuring quantities of goods which are broadly similar, simple aggregation is often used. (Steel output is measured by tonnes of steel produced and car output by number of cars, despite the fact that a Mini is very different from a Rolls Royce.) But where very different items are aggregated, some form of weighting is needed. The most common systems used are again derived from Laspeyres and Paasche. The Laspeyres quantity index, J^L_t, is constructed by weighting the quantities by base period prices, $J^L_t = \Sigma q_t p_0 / \Sigma q_0 p_0$, while the Paasche index is calculated using current prices as weights, $J^P_t = \Sigma q_t p_t / \Sigma q_0 p_t$. Since the quantities will tend to be largest for those goods whose prices have risen least, if one is constructing an index of national output, for example, the Laspeyres index will again exceed the Paasche index.

But neither index is completely satisfactory. For multiplying a Laspeyres price index by the same quantity index does not yield the ratio of current to base period values. Instead one must multiply the Paasche price index by the Laspeyres quantity index to obtain the ratio of values. In order to remedy this and a number of other defects, various combinations of the two have been proposed, although these are not greatly used in practice.

Nevertheless the theoretical development of index numbers has continued. Thus Barnett (1981) deals with the problem of constructing a quantity index of monetary aggregates. Allen (1975) provides a detailed reference on index numbers, while the work of Diewert (1976) and Afriat (1977) contributes further theoretical development of the subject.

Martin Weale
University of Cambridge

References

Afriat, S. N. (1977), *The Price Index*, Cambridge.

Allen, R. D. G. (1975), *Index Numbers in Theory and Practice*, Chicago.

Barnett, W. A. (1981), 'Economic monetary aggregates: an application of index number theory', *Journal of Econometrics (Supplement)*.

Diewart, W. E. (1976), 'Exact and superlative index numbers', *Journal of Econometrics*.

Interviews and Interviewing

The use of surveys in social science research has expanded considerably in the last three decades, and with it the practice of interviewing. The interview is one of the most central parts of the survey-taking process: it is the source of information for the researcher who has carefully designed and integrated the components of a survey. A well-designed survey starts with an overall study design, a sample that fits the needs of the survey, a carefully drafted questionnaire, editing and coding rules to summarize the data collected, and an analysis plan. But even if these pieces are executed flawlessly, any survey can be a failure if the interviewing is poorly handled. The increased use of interviews has led to the development of multiple interviewing techniques, an improvement in methods used by interviewers, and the establishment of trained permanent staffs to conduct interviews.

Types of Interviews

In survey research, there are essentially three techniques for gathering information from respondents: mail, telephone, and personal interviews. The choice between these techniques depends on the money and time available for collecting information, the types of questions being asked, and concerns about data quality. Mail interviews are usually conducted with a small to moderate length questionnaire; questions asked in a mail questionnaire should not be especially difficult and there should be relatively few places in the questionnaire where the respondent has to 'skip' to a different series of questions. Mail interviews are the cheapest of the methods used for interviewing, but in using them the researcher gives up control over the interview process. In a carefully designed study, research should be conducted under controlled conditions so that no factors extraneous to the topic being studied can intrude on the data collection. In the case of a mail interview, the researcher cannot determine who will fill out the questionnaire if sent to a home or business, nor can he use probing type statements to obtain more detailed answers to complex questions.

Telephone interviews resolve some of these problems. The interviewer can to some degree control who responds to the questions and can probe to obtain clarification of ambiguous responses. These interviews can be more detailed than mail interviews and more complicated questionnaire designs are possible, since the telephone interviewer can be trained in how the questionnaire should be completed. One disadvantage is that telephone interviews must be kept somewhat short, usually one-half hour or less, to avoid respondent fatigue; they also cost more than mail interviews – interviewers must be paid, and there are capital costs for telephone equipment and use.

As in the case of mail and telephone interviews, personal interviews have their trade-offs. Personal interviews can be substantially more expensive than telephone interviews because of the travel costs. But there are advantages: a much more detailed and lengthy interview can be conducted with a respondent; the personal interview allows the interviewer to use printed materials like flash cards to elicit responses; the interviewer is also able to see and interact with the respondent, which can be a help in determining whether the respondent is confused by, or bored with, the questions being asked. This mode allows the interviewer the most control over the interview process.

Ranking the three methods by cost, the mail interview is least expensive, followed by telephone and then personal interviews. There are exceptions to this ordering that depend on the circumstances of the survey. But in terms of the quality of the data, the interviewer has more control of and can ask more detailed questions in a personal interview. Telephone interviews offer some control of the interview, though less than the personal, and mail interviews offer the least control and the least opportunity for asking detailed questions. Again, this ranking will not always hold true, as there are circumstances and types of questions where the respondent will be more comfortable in responding by telephone or mail because of embarrassment or discomfort in talking to a stranger.

Another factor affecting the choice between the three interviewing modes is response rates. Responses to mail surveys have traditionally been lower than those obtained for telephone or personal interview surveys. This has led to the practice of mixed mode surveys, with an initial or multiple attempts to contact respondents by mail, followed by telephone and personal contacts to increase response.

Methods of Interviewing
As in any area of scientific inquiry, the data collected in a survey need to be of the highest quality to enable the researcher to draw from them. Errors in the data, especially biases due to flaws in the collection process, can lead to erroneous conclusions in analysis. To improve further the quality of survey data, several modifications to the interview process have been introduced that increase response and enhance quality.

Two examples of these types of modifications will illustrate such improvements. The first is the use of diaries; in a broad range of surveys, from consumer behaviour to epidemiological studies, diaries have been introduced to improve the quality of the data gathered. Surveys that ask retrospective questions about behaviour frequently have problems with recall loss, that is, the respondent cannot remember all instances of a given action. To help the respondent, it is now a common practice to have an interviewer collect demographic and attitudinal information during a personal visit interview, and to leave a diary to be filled out by the respondent on a daily basis which would describe the type of behaviour being studied over a week or longer. This methodology has been especially useful in consumption studies and research on time usage.

A second method used for interviewing is an enhancement to the telephone interview. Traditional methods for interviewing have used paper questionnaires with the interviewer transcribing responses. The new method, computer-assisted telephone interviewing (CATI), uses the computer to give the interviewer questions on a display screen, and the interviewer types in the respondent's answers to be stored in computer memory. The computer controls the interview, using the responses to determine how to branch through skip patterns and providing some editing of data for inconsistent responses. Although the initial investment can be high, CATI allows for better control of the survey and leads to better quality in the data collected.

The Interviewer

General survey practice for large and moderate-sized survey organizations has been to hire and train permanent interviewing staffs. The interviewer is recognized as a skilled professional who contributes to the survey effort through his experience in contacting respondents, conducting interviews, and understanding what the researcher is attempting to study. In most survey organizations, the interviewer as a permanent staff member receives training in these skills, in methods for asking and coding questions, and in general principles of the conduct of a survey interview. For particular studies, the interviewer will receive training as to the intent of each question and the study as a whole, how to deal with difficult skip patterns, and other information relevant to the study. Many organizations have two interviewing staffs, one trained exclusively for telephone interviewing from a central location, the other a geographically dispersed group of interviewers who conduct personal interviews. These would be trained and supervised differently, since the interviewing techniques would be different.

Charles D. Cowan
Bureau of the Census
United States Department of Commerce

Further Reading

Bradburn, N. M. and Sudman, S. (1979), *Improving Interview Method and Questionnaire Design*, San Francisco.

Cannell, C. F., Oksenberg, L. and Converse, J. M. (1979), *Experiments in Interviewing Techniques*, Ann Arbor.

Gorden, R. (1975), *Interviewing: Strategy, Techniques and Tactics*, Homewood, Ill.

Hoinville, G., Jowell, R. and Associates (1978), *Survey Research Practices*, London.

Smith, J. M. (1972), *Interviewing in Market and Social Research*, London.

See also: *questionnaires; sample surveys.*

Kuhn, Thomas Samuel (1922–)

Thomas Kuhn, born in Cincinnati, Ohio in 1922, was trained as a theoretical physicist, but it was his experience teaching a course in the theory and practice of science for non-scientists that first undermined his preconceptions about science and the reasons for its special success. Under the influence of J. B. Conant at Harvard (where Kuhn took his degree), Kuhn began to explore the divergence between the idealized accounts of science produced by philosophers and the reality unearthed by research into its historical development. His subsequent work can be seen as a consistent attempt to bring the former into line with the latter. It is therefore clear why, with these preoccupations, Kuhn is one of the few historians of science to produce a general model of science.

His most influential book is *The Structure of Scientific Revolutions* (1970), first published in 1962, in which science is portrayed as an activity bound by precedent and tradition. Scientific contributions are modelled on past achievements. These exemplary achievements Kuhn calls 'paradigms'. Paradigms are not simply theories but pieces of work which embody all the elements of scientific practice within some specialized area of inquiry. They exhibit the important parameters to be measured, define required standards of accuracy, show how observations are to be interpreted and the kind of experimental methods to be used. An example is John Dalton's *New System of Chemical Philosophy*, published in 1808, which showed how to understand chemical reactions in terms of atom to atom linkages, and how to make inferences about atoms by measuring the relative weights of combining substances. Paradigms leave many problems unsolved, and hence allow the growth of research traditions in which their concepts are refined to account for new results and applications. Kuhn calls this process of articulation and exploitation 'normal science', because it is what most scientists do most of the time. Normal science is a creative form of puzzle solving, whose difficulties are seen as tests of the ingenuity of the scientist rather than tests of the truth of the paradigm. Kuhn then argues that it is this very commitment of scientists to their paradigm that eventually brings about its overthrow. As it is pressed into service in ever more detail, the expectation of success sensitizes scientists to failures. If experimental results continue to resist explanation in terms of the accepted paradigm, a crisis of confidence may ensue. A new approach based on a new paradigmatic achievement may gain favour if it appears to resolve the difficulty and opens up new lines of puzzle-solving activity. This constitutes a revolution, but the rejected paradigm will not have been decisively proven false, because no one knows what greater persistence with it might have revealed. The cycle of paradigm, normal science and revolution then repeats itself.

Kuhn's picture has two important consequences:
(1) Scientific knowledge cannot be simply 'read-off' from nature: it is always mediated by historically specific and culturally shared paradigms. This challenges our intuitions about scientific truth and progress.
(2) Neither continuity nor change in science can be understood by means of abstract rules. The coherence of normal science derives from the family resemblances between work modelled on a paradigm, and the change of paradigm requires an intuitive judgement that cannot be fully justified by abstract and independent principles. Not surprisingly Kuhn has been charged with 'irrationalism', though he is really only challenging certain philosophical preconceptions about rationality. His position has affinities with Wittgenstein's, because we can say that each paradigm gives rise to a particular 'language-game'. In conjunction with Kuhn's stress on tradition, commitment and precedent, this explains why his work has proved an important stimulus and resource for studies in the sociology of science.

In 1961, Kuhn took up a professorship in the history of

science at the University of California, Berkeley, and in 1964 he moved to Princeton University.

David Bloor
University of Edinburgh

Reference
Kuhn, T. S. (1977), *The Structure of Scientific Revolutions*, 2nd edn, Chicago.

Further Reading
Barnes, B. (1982), *T. S. Kuhn and Social Science*, London.
Fleck, L. (1979), *Genesis and Development of a Scientific Fact*, Chicago. (First published in German in 1935.) (A pioneering book in the sociology of knowledge which anticipated many of the themes in Kuhn's work and to which Kuhn was himself indebted.)
Kuhn, T. S. (1957), *The Copernican Revolution*, Cambridge, Mass.
Kuhn, T. S. (1977), *The Essential Tension: Selected Studies in Scientific Tradition and Change*, Chicago.
Kuhn, T. S. (1978), *Black Body Theory and the Quantum Discontinuity, 1894–1912*, Oxford.

Life Histories

A life history may be defined as the sequence of events and experiences in a life from birth until death. Life histories can be studied not only with the 'life history method' of having a respondent recount the story of his or her life, but also with the full range of social-scientific and historical methods, including archival research, participant observation, experimental methods, and longitudinal research.

Within the social sciences, it is possible to identify roughly three periods in the study of life histories:

(1) From approximately 1920 to the Second World War, there was a substantial and growing interest in life histories, much of it associated with the study of personal documents such as autobiographies, letters and diaries (Thomas and Znaniecki, 1920; Murray, 1938; Allport, 1942). (2) From the Second World

War to the mid-1960s, interest declined and instead increased attention was given to more structured quantitative and experimental methods. (3) However, within the last two decades, there has been an enormous outpouring of work in the study of lives associated with developments in fields such as life-history research in psychopathology (Roff and Ricks, 1970), adult development (Levinson *et al.*, 1978; White, 1975), sociological studies of the life course (Elder, 1974), oral history and life stories (Bennett, 1981; Bertaux,1981), and psychobiography (Erikson, 1975; Runyan, 1982).

Critics argue that life-history studies are ineffective in ruling out competing causal explanations and that it is unsafe to generalize from the study of a single case. Studies of individual life histories are, however, appropriately evaluated not on their effectiveness for testing causal generalizations (a criterion most appropriate for experimental studies), but rather on their ability to present and interpret information about the life of a single individual. Such studies can usefully be evaluated through a 'quasi-judicial' methodology (Bromley, 1977), analogous to procedures in courts of law, where evidence, inferences and interpretations in a life-history study are critically assessed by those with competing points of view who are free to present their own evidence, interpretations and conclusions.

The goals of psychology can be thought of as existing on three distinct levels: learning (1) what is true of persons-in-general; (2) what is true of groups of persons, distinguished by sex, race, social class, culture and historical period; and (3) what is true of individual human beings. These three levels of analysis inform one another, but are also partially independent. The study of individual life histories is a necessary complement to the study of group differences and the search for universal generalizations.

William McKinley Runyan
University of California, Berkeley

References
Allport, G. W. (1942), *The Use of Personal Documents in Psychological Science*, New York.

Bennett, J. (1981), *Oral History and Delinquency: The Rhetoric of Criminology*, Chicago.

Bertaux, D. (ed.) (1981), *Biography and Society: The Life History Approach in the Social Sciences*, Beverly Hills, Calif.

Bromley, D. B. (1977), *Personality Description in Ordinary Language*, New York.

Elder, G. H., Jr (1974), *Children of the Great Depression*, Chicago.

Erikson, E. H. (1975), *Life History and the Historical Moment*, New York.

Levinson, D. *et al.* (1978), *The Seasons of a Man's Life*, New York.

Murray, H. A. *et al.* (1938), *Explorations in Personality*, New York.

Roff, M. and Ricks, D. (eds) (1970), *Life History Research in Psychopathology*, vol. I, Minneapolis.

Runyan, W. M. (1982), *Life Histories and Psychobiography: Explorations in Theory and Method*, New York.

White, R. W. (1975), *Lives in Progress*, 3rd edn, New York.

Thomas, W. I. and Znaniecki, F. (1920), *The Polish Peasant in Europe and America*, Boston.

See also: *case studies*.

Marketing Research

The purpose of marketing research is to provide information which will aid in management decision making. A marketing manager in a large consumer goods company, for example, may want to collect information to assess whether or not to launch a new product or to determine why sales of a product are declining. In collecting this information, five major steps may be identified: (1) establishment of research objectives; (2) development of a research plan; (3) implementation of the research plan; (4) data analysis; and (5) presentation of research findings (Churchill, 1983; Green and Tull, 1978; Lehmann, 1983).

(1) Establishment of Research Objectives
This is the first step, and it requires clear and precise definition by management of the decision problem. This should be expressed not only in terms of problem symptoms such as a decline in market share, but also possible contributing factors such as

changes in competitors' strategies or in consumer interests, as well as the actions management might take based on research findings. Otherwise, much irrelevant information may be collected.

(2) Development of a Research Plan

This stage requires determining what data are to be collected, what research techniques and instruments are to be used, how the sample is to be selected, and how information is to be collected from this sample.

(i)   *Data sources*: The required information may already be available in *secondary* sources such as government or trade reports, company records, or sales-force reports. This will not, however, have been collected with this particular problem in mind. Consequently, *primary* data collection may be required, in other words, collection of information specifically for this purpose.

(ii) *Research techniques*: Where primary data are collected, observational or other qualitative techniques, experimentation or survey research may be conducted. *Observational* and other qualitative techniques, such as projective techniques, (word association or sentence completion tasks, and focus or group interviewing) are most appropriate in the initial stages of research, where little is known about the problem (Webb, Campbell, Schwartz and Sechrest, 1966). The onus of interpretation is, however, placed on the researcher, and, consequently, such techniques are open to criticisms of subjectivity. *Experimental* techniques are also potentially applicable, but they are rarely used except in in-store experiments, studying, for example, the impact of in-store promotions on sales. Test marketing can also be viewed as field experiments. *Survey* research is the technique most commonly used in marketing research. A standard questionnaire can be administered to large samples, and systematically analysed using computerized techniques.

(iii) *Research instruments*: In observational or qualitative research, instruments such as coding schema, recording sheets and other tests may need to be designed. Mechanical devices such as instruments to measure a subject's eye movements or pupil dilation, or optical scanner equipment are also increasingly used. But more common is the questionnaire. For unstructured interviews and focus groups, only an interview guide indicating the topics to be covered may be required. A crucial aspect of survey research is, however, the design of a questionnaire carefully worded to elicit desired information from respondents (Oppenheim, 1966; Payne, 1951). Attention to question form and sequencing is also often essential in order to avoid biased responses.

(iv) *Sampling plan*: This should specify the sample population, its size and sampling procedures to be adopted. The relevant sample population and sample size will depend on the purpose of the research, and the research budget. In qualitative research, small samples are common, but more extensive surveys often require a large sample size. A choice has also to be made between probabilistic sampling techniques, such as random or stratified sampling, and non-probabilistic sampling techniques such as judgemental, quota or convenience sampling (Cochran, 1977). Probability sampling is the only way to obtain a representative sample but requires the availability of a sampling list and entails high costs. Convenience, judgemental or quota sampling techniques are thus often used, particularly where qualitative techniques are applied, or a specific target segment is to be studied.

(v) *Data collection procedures*: Three principal methods of data collection may be considered: telephone, mail or personal interviewing. *Telephone* interviewing, which is commonly used in the US, is quick and can be conducted from a central location where interviewers are controlled by a supervisor. However, only those with telephones can be interviewed, and a limited number of questions asked. *Mail* questionnaires are the cheapest method of survey administration, but suffer from low response rates, and also assume that the respondent clearly understands and can respond to questions. *Personal* interviewing is the most flexible method since the interviewer can select the sample by judgement or convenience sampling, and is able to explain questions to the respondent. It is, however, an expensive method of data collection, and susceptible to interviewer bias.

(3) Implementation of the Research Plan

This is where major sources of data inaccuracy and unreliability often arise. In the case of surveys, for example, respondents may bias findings by refusal to co-operate, by providing inaccurate answers, for example on income, or by giving socially desirable responses. Interviewers may also bias results by encouraging a specific response, by inaccurate recording of responses or, in extreme cases, by falsifying responses.

Current developments in telecommunications and computer technology are rapidly changing data collection procedures and improving their efficiency. For example, in both centralized telephone interviewing and in mobile field units, computer terminals can be used by interviewers or interviewees to record responses, thereby eliminating editing and coding errors. The results can also be analysed and updated with each successive response, thus considerably reducing research time and costs.

(4) Data Analysis

The next step is to tabulate, classify, and interpret the information collected. Here, the complexity of the analysis will depend to a large extent on management needs. In many cases, tabulation or cross-tabulation of results with averages and other summary statistics may suffice. In other cases, more sophisticated multivariate techniques such as factor or cluster analysis or multidimensional scaling may be required, if more complex interactions in the data are to be examined (Green, 1978).

(5) Presentation of Research Findings

Presentation of research findings may be verbal and/or written. In either case, the main focus should be on clear presentation of key research findings and their implications for the decisions to be made by management.

Susan P. Douglas
New York University

References

Churchill, G. (1983), *Marketing Research*, 3rd edn, Hinsdale, Ill.

Cochran, W. G. (1977), *Sampling Techniques*, 3rd edn, New York.

Green, P. E. (1978), *Analyzing Multivariate Data*, Hinsdale, Ill.

Green, P. E. and Tull, D. S. (1978), *Research for Marketing Decisions*, 4th edn, Englewood Cliffs, N.J.

Lehmann, D. (1983), *Market Research and Analysis*, 2nd edn, Homewood, Ill.

Oppenheim, A. N. (1966), *Questionnaire Design and Attitude Measurement*, New York.

Payne, S. (1951), *The Art of Asking Questions*, Princeton.

Webb, E., Campbell, D. T., Schwartz, R. D. and Sechrest, L. (1966), *Unobtrusive Measures*, Chicago.

Further Reading

Baker, M. J. (ed.) (1983), *Marketing: Theory and Practice*, 3rd edn, London.

See also: *opinion polls; sample surveys.*

Mathematical Models

As mathematics is a powerful, flexible language and models are representations, mathematical models are representations framed in mathematical terms. A good metaphor for a mathematical model is a map. A map is a simple device for representing a complex geographical locality. Much of the 'richness' of the locality is removed in the representation but enough remains for it to be recognized. Whether the map is a good one depends not only on its properties but also on the use to which it is put. If you want to get through a city quickly, a simple map of the arterial routes suffices. For a walking tour of a city centre, a detailed map of the city centre is enough, and if you are hiking in open country a geological survey map works fine – if you know how to use it. Much the same applies to mathematical models: they are representations for a purpose and some knowledge is required to build and use them.

First, the purposes: construction of social science theory entails a concern with, among other things, generality, precision, and parsimony. In place of scattered ideographic propositions, a concern for generality pushes us towards nomothetic propositions that link into coherent and powerful theories of social phenomena. Mathematics has a role in both the formulation of these propositions and their linkage. Given a concern for precision we need to know what we measure, the error bounds of our tools, that our measurement produces high-quality data good enough to support propositions, and that our propositions say exactly what we mean and not some vague approximation. Mathematics can help the construction of measurement tools, the analysis of the properties of these measurement tools and the statement of precise propositions. Parsimony implies a concern for theoretical efficiency: if a simple theory adequately explains phenomena, there is no need for a complex one. Mathematical formulations facilitate the construction of simple theories and make clear the assumptions underlying the construction of theories (which are very important, even if unacknowledged, components of a theory).

Just as it would be folly to claim that generality, precision, and parsimony are all that matter in theory construction, so would it be folly to claim that mathematics is the only way, or even the best way, to achieve these ends. It is one way: a language with tools and techniques that may prove useful.

Second, the knowledge (skill) required for mathematical model building is easily stated. It includes good intuitions, and ability to abstract, some knowledge of a range of models, some facility with the manipulation of the mathematical representations (that is, derivation of logical consequences), an ability to assess critically the models, some flair, and modesty.

We now consider model building which is done within some broad methodology (Doreian and Hummon, 1976) having epistemological, substantive, technical and purposive components. Within the epistemological component, criteria for the construction and evaluation of models are set forth. Within the substantive component, the nature of the theory, its theoretical terms and the nature of relevant data are formulated. The technical component deals with the nuts and bolts of modelling – the mathematical systems used, their properties, measurement and estimation. Within the purposive component we can discuss the goals of the modelling effort. These include explanation, description and explication. They also include a consideration of the uses of a model. Of course, these components are highly interrelated. A model must have a clear set of criteria for evaluating its knowledge claims, make substantive sense, and be technically adequate. Additionally, the model may lead to identification of modes of implementation and intervention.

Discussions of mathematical models are frequently co-ordinated by at least two of the following distinctions. The first differentiates process models from structural models, the second deterministic models from probabilistic (stochastic) models, and the third differentiates models using discrete variables from those using continuous variables. In principle, an eight-cell table can be constructed using these three criteria and each cell filled with mathematical models sharing the criteria defining the cell.

Models of processes explicitly attempt to model change and provide an understanding of the mechanisms of change. Among the frequently used tools are differential equations and difference equations. Models of structure attempt to represent and understand the structure of social relations. Frequently used mathematical tools include graph theory and matrix algebra; in addition, modern algebraic tools such as groups, semi-groups and Boolean algebras find applications in these structural analyses, as well as category theory and algebraic topology.

Stochastic models are used to model processes whose outcomes are governed by a probabilistic mechanism(s). Many types of stochastic models are available to social scientists (see Bartholomew, 1982). Deterministic models eschew stochastic mechanisms in favour of deterministic mechanisms and relations. The process models of social change can be deterministic or stochastic. The structural models tend to be deterministic. If the models are discrete they use variables that can only take one of the small number of states, whereas continuous models use variables that are, or can be, treated usefully as if they are continuous. For the process models, a further distinction can be made concerning the representation of time: it, too, can be taken as discrete or continuous.

Mathematical models have wide-ranging applications in the

social sciences. (For many examples see Fararo (1973), Rapoport (1983) and Sørensen (1978).) A modeller selects the mathematical model best suited for a substantive problem where skill shows in knowledge of alternative model candidates and selection of the most fruitful one(s). Mathematical modellers tend to draw on mathematics already developed using models formulated in other disciplines. This is unproblematic if the model captures the crucial theoretical aspects, and critical empirical components, of the substantive problem. Indeed, mathematical models draw their power from being devoid of substantive content: a mathematical model can be used fruitfully in different areas of one field or even in different fields. Seldom have mathematics been invented because of social science needs, which contrasts with the physical science tradition exemplified by the invention of the differential-integral calculus by Newton and Leibniz. Exceptions include game theory, decision theory and some areas of artificial intelligence research. So much for models, but what is a good model?

Good models must be adequate in all components of its methodology. The Theory-Model-Data triangle of Leik and Meeker (1975) provides a way of discussing this. There are three pairs of mappings – between theory and model; between model and data; and between theory and data – and all are important (although different model builders may place differential emphasis on them).

The theory-model linkage is concerned with expressing a congruence between a theory and its representation in a mathematical model. The theory has to map into the model with little distortion or loss. Deductively, there is a mathematical formalization of the theory while, inductively, this can be a formal generalization of the theory. The mathematical model then has to be useful. Useful, here, means the machinery of the mathematical system has to be mobilized to derive or establish mathematical results. These results can be mapped to the theory and to the data. Deductively, the model maps to the (empirical) data by specifying, or predicting, empirical outcomes. The model is truly predictive if it makes predictions that can be checked empirically. Sometimes models are not predictive in this sense. Instead they lead to the construction of descriptions based on data. Also deductively, the mathematical results (theorems) map to the theory by specifying the theoretical implications of the derivations through the mappings linking theory and model.

When the empirical predictions and specifications stemming from the model are confronted with data, several outcomes are possible: (1) The predictions made on the basis of the theory and the model may be borne out, providing support for the model. The results are filtered back through the mappings and interpreted substantively. (2) If a model calls only for empirical descriptions, these by themselves are not, at face value, too important. However, they must make sense when interpreted theoretically. (3) The model may lead to predictions that are disconfirmed, calling the model into question. The model builder then has to establish if the model should be rebuilt or discarded. This requires skill. Further, this decision has other important implications: measurements must be good and empirical evidence is decisive. Which brings us to statistical methodology.

The frequently made distinction between mathematical models and statistical analysis is a very blurred one. Formal approaches can, and do, incorporate error specification (a theory of error) — which other approaches generally do not. This informs estimation. Second, the properties of the statistical tools are stated and established mathematically. Finally, new mathematical models and their uses generate estimation problems and statistical questions.

Space precludes discussion of the rest of the Theory-Model-Data triangle but each does constrain the others. The theory, the model, and the data have to make sense and be consistent with one another — which is the nub of evaluating models.

The charge is often made that mathematical models overlook much of the richness and texture of social life. They do, and this is a virtue (which is not to say that richness and texture are irrelevant). The claim that social phenomena are incredibly complex and that this complexity cannot be captured via mathematical models need not detain us. While the basic laws of physics are simple, for example Newton's laws of motion, they generate behaviours that are, and appear to observers as, very complex. Note also that complex mathematical formulae are generated from 'simple' start points. A direct attempt to model the complexity, for example to predict the exact trajectory of a snowflake in a storm or a leaf in a wind, would appear bizarre and fruitless. Yet in the social sciences there are many attempts to 'model', in one way or another, the surface phenomena of human life. Following the distinction between noise and true signals, the modeller and the critic need to evaluate the model on the basis of (good) measurement of signals rather than of noise. While empirical evidence is decisive, not all measurements count. That social behaviour is complex cannot be denied, but the principles governing this behaviour need not be complex. They may even permit a mathematical description (which does not mean we have slavishly to follow the mathematical antics of the natural sciences – or even use the same mathematics). In this context, computer simulation models are used fruitfully.

It does not follow that all social scientists should use mathematics, only that some do. While mathematical models are used quite frequently, only a minority of social scientists create and use them. Yet, even so, we can point to a powerful drive towards mathematical expression of and solutions to disciplinary and, more strongly, interdisciplinary problems. Social science publications like *The Journal of Mathematical Sociology* and *The Journal of Mathematical Psychology* find counterparts among the natural sciences in *The Journal of Mathematical Physics* and *Mathematical Geology*. Of course, neither set validates the other. There are many publications without mathematics in their title but which, nevertheless, carry a heavy mathematical imprint. These include *Psychometrika*, *Sociological Methodology*, *Social Networks*, *Geographical Analysis*, *Econometrica* and *Environment and Planning*. Within all of these journals good mathematical social science can be found. What is less clear is whether all of this activity stems from an intrinsic need for the use of mathematics in a discipline at a certain stage, or crude imitation between fields, or even the carving out of a niche by the mathematically inclined. Probably a bit of each is involved, but while imitation and niche creation are not intellectually illegitimate, only the first provides the continuing basis and context for significant work.

The mathematically inclined members of the social science tribe talk largely to themselves, primarily because they have learned the language, but also because many other tribe members do not care to listen. To the extent that the mathematical folk are concerned only to build their models for the sake of building them, they will remain in their intellectual niche. This will change only with the construction of powerful and relevant (hence successful) mathematical models. Then, perhaps, the niche will expand to form the ecosystem.

Patrick Doreian
University of Pittsburgh

References

Bartholomew, D. J. (1982), *Stochastic Models for Social Processes*, 3rd edn, New York.

Doreian, P. and Hummon, N. P. (1976), *Modelling Social Processes*, New York.

Fararo, T. (1973), *Mathematical Sociology: An Introduction to Fundamentals*, New York.

Leik, R. K. and Meeker, B. F. (1975), *Mathematical Sociology*, Englewood Cliffs, N.J.

Rapoport, A. (1983), *Mathematical Models in the Social and Behavioural Sciences*, New York.

Sørensen, A. (1978), 'Mathematical models in sociology', *Annual Review of Sociology*, 4.

Further Reading

Coleman, J. S. (1964), *An Introduction to Mathematical Sociology*, New York.

See also: *catastrophe theory; computer simulation; game theory; graph theory; path analysis.*

Measures of Central Tendency and Dispersion

(1) Suppose n observations – or measurements – are collected on some variable, such observations could be characterized by a measure of their *central tendency*. It is defined as follows: replace

all observations by an identical number $\bar{x}$. Obviously, this implies loss of information. Therefore $\bar{x}$ must be chosen in such a way that loss is minimized. This, in turn, requires a definition of loss. One possibility is to define loss as the average absolute difference between $\bar{x}$ and all individual observations:

$$s = \Sigma |x_i - \bar{x}| \; n \qquad (i=1, \ldots, n)$$

Obviously, this measure of loss is a measure of *dispersion*: its value is small if all observations are close to $\bar{x}$, and becomes larger to the extent individual observations have a greater distance from $\bar{x}$. With loss defined in this way, it becomes minimized by setting $\bar{x}$ equal to the *median* (that is, $\bar{x}$ must be chosen in such a way that there are as many individual observations larger than $\bar{x}$ as smaller than $\bar{x}$). A simple example (see also Table 1) is that $n = 5$ observations are collected with values (1 1 2 4 7). The median equals 2 (there are two observations larger than 2, and also two observations smaller than 2). Absolute differences between the five observations and $\bar{x} = 2$ are equal to (1 1 0 2 5), with average $s = 9/5 = 1.8$. This value is smaller than for any other choice of $\bar{x}$.

Table 1

	x_i	1	1	2	4	7	15
	$|x_i - \bar{x}|^0$	0	0	1	1	1	3
$\bar{x} = 1$	$|x_i - \bar{x}|^1$	0	0	1	3	6	10
	$|x_i - \bar{x}|^2$	0	0	1	9	36	46
	$|x_i - \bar{x}|^0$	1	1	0	1	1	4
$\bar{x} = 2$	$|x_i - \bar{x}|^1$	1	1	0	2	5	9
	$|x_i - \bar{x}|^2$	1	1	0	4	25	31
	$|x_i - \bar{x}|^0$	1	1	1	1	1	5
$\bar{x} = 3$	$|x_i - \bar{x}|^1$	2	2	1	1	4	10
	$|x_i - \bar{x}|^2$	4	4	1	1	16	26
	$|x_i - \bar{x}|^0$	1	1	1	0	1	4
$\bar{x} = 4$	$|x_i - \bar{x}|^1$	3	3	2	0	3	11
	$|x_i - \bar{x}|^2$	9	9	4	0	9	31

The table shows powers ($p = 0, 1, 2$) of absolute differences between observed values x_i and $\bar{x}$, with $\bar{x}$ running from 1 to 4. For $\bar{x} = 1$ (mode) the sum of the powers with $p = 0$ is minimized.
For $\bar{x} = 2$ (median) the sum of the powers with $p = 1$ is minimized.
For $\bar{x} = 3$ (mean) the sum of the powers with $p = 2$ is minimized.
For $\bar{x} = 4$ (midrange) the pth root of the sum of the powers with $p \to \infty$ would become minimized at the value 3 (not shown in table).

Another possibility is to define loss as the average squared difference between $\bar{x}$ and all individual observations:

$$s = \Sigma(x_i - \bar{x})^2/n$$

To minimize this loss function, $\bar{x}$ must be set equal to the (arithmetic) *mean* of the observations. In the example above, the mean equals $15/5 = 3$. Squared differences between individual observations and the mean are equal to (4 4 1 1 16) with average $s = 26/5 = 5.2$. This is smaller than for any other choice of $\bar{x}$. Again, the average squared distance between mean and individual observations is a measure of dispersion; it is called the *variance*.

A third possible choice for the measure of central tendency is the *mode*. It is defined as the value with the largest frequency. In the example above the mode is equal to 1. Loss now must be defined as the proportion of observations not in the category with largest frequency. In the example this proportion is equal to $3/5 = .6$; it is smaller than for any other choice of $\bar{x}$ And, again, this proportion is a (crude) measure of dispersion.

(2) Results obtained above can be unified by defining loss as

$$s = \{\Sigma|x_i - \bar{x}|^p/n\}^{1/p}$$

With $p = 0$, s is minimized by taking $\bar{x}$ equal to the mode.
With $p = 1$, s is minimized by setting $\bar{x}$ equal to the median.
With $p = 2$, s is minimized by taking $\bar{x}$ equal to the mean.
With p very large ($p \to \sim$) it can be shown that s is minimized by setting $\bar{x}$ equal to the *mid-range* (the average of largest and

smallest observation; in the example the mid-range is equal to $(7 + 1)/2 = 4$. In that case s becomes equal to half the *range*, where the range is defined as the difference between largest and smallest observation (in the example, the range equals $7 - 1 = 6$, so that s, with very large p, becomes equal to 3).

(3) The choice between mode, median, or mean is related to the level of *measurement* of the observations. At the *nominal* level, numbers are used only as labels for different categories, such as in a hardware shop where box 1 contains nails, box 2 contains screws, box 3 bolts, and box 4 tacks. The mode makes sense: it identifies the category with largest frequency. The median makes sense if observations are on an *ordinal* level: numbers not only label categories but also impose a certain order upon them. The mean requires *interval scale* level of measurement – it assumes that differences between numerical values have meaningful interpretation. On *ratio scale* level – where ratios between numerical values have meaningful interpretation and where it is assumed that all numerical values are non-negative – another measure of central tendency might make sense: it is the *geometric mean*, defined as the nth root of the product of all observations. In the example above the geometric mean would be equal to $(56) 1/5 = 2.24$.

(4) For symmetric distributions, mode, median, and mean will have identical value. A distribution is said to be skewed to the right if mode < median < mean, and skewed to the left if mode > median > mean.

(5) If the n observations can be interpreted as a random sample from some population with mean equal to μ, the sample mean $\bar{x}$ is said to be an *estimate* of μ. Moreover, $\bar{x}$ is an *unbiased* estimate, which just says that with n very large, the sample mean approximates the population mean. If the population has symmetric distribution, sample median and sample mode also are unbiased estimates of the population mean. However, sample means then fluctuate around the population mean with less variance than sample medians, or sample modes. Therefore the sample mean is said to be an *efficient* estimate of the population mean, whereas sample median or sample mode are not efficient estimates.

(6) The argument in sections (1) and (2) above imply that

choice of a measure of central tendency is intimately related to choice of a measure of loss, or dispersion. But in economics and sociology another measure of dispersion was popular, called the *Gini-index*. It is defined as the average of the absolute differences between all pairs of observations:

$$G = \Sigma |x_i - x_j|/n^2.$$

In this definition, differences between each observation and itself are included – such differences are zero, of course. Sometimes the Gini-index is defined with $n(n - 1)$ in the denominator instead of n^2; differences between each observation and itself are then not counted.

The Gini-index is seemingly independent of the choice of a measure of central tendency, as if it measures 'intrinsic' dispersion. This is not true, however. The Gini-index concentrates on absolute differences, and has the same 'philosophy' about loss as the median. This becomes more clear if a revised Gini-index is defined as the average of the squared differences between all pairs of observations. The index then becomes equal to twice the variance. Although it looks as if dispersion is measured 'intrinsically', there is no escape: a measure for dispersion implies a measure for central tendency, and vice versa.

John van de Geer
University of Leiden

See also: *multivariate analysis; statistical reasoning*.

Multivariate Analysis

(1) Multivariate analysis (MVA) is defined here as the analysis of data collected in a matrix with n rows and m columns, in such a way that columns refer to m variables, whereas rows refer to the objects measured. For example, the columns might stand for economic variables (GNP, export/import trade balance, percentage unemployed, and so on) and the row for different countries for which the economic measurements have been collected.

MVA may serve many purposes, the most general of which is to obtain *clarification* of the data, usually in the form of *data reduction*. More specific purposes are the analysis of *dependence* (whether variance of some variables can be 'explained' by co-variance with other variables), and *classification* of objects into subgroups.

(2) The simplest example of dependence analysis is *multiple regression* where the variance of a single variable y is related to that of a number of variables $x_1, x_2, \ldots, x_m$. The basic objective of the analysis is to identify regression weights for the variables x_t, in such a way that their weighted sum has maximum correlation with y. This correlation is called the *multiple correlation coefficient*. A generalization is that there are two or more dependent variables $y_1, y_2, \ldots$. In this case one should also solve for weights for these dependent variables, in such a way that their weighted sum has optimal correlation with a weighted sum of the independent variables $x_1, x_2, \ldots$. Such correlations are called *canonical correlations*.

Dependence analysis may appear in many different guises. One of these is *analysis of variance*, where observations on a single dependent variable y are collected under a variety of experimental conditions. These conditions divide objects into subgroups. They can be coded in an *indicator matrix*. The first column x_1 of this matrix will have entries 1 for all objects in the first condition, and entries zero otherwise. The second column x_2 will have entries 1 for all objects in the second condition, zero otherwise, and so on. Formally, the problem to be solved then becomes the same as in multiple correlation: to find out to what extent y depends on the variables $x_1, x_2 \ldots$, or combinations of them. In *multivariate analysis of variance* there are two or more dependent variables $y_1, x_2, \ldots$ The problem then becomes formally the same as in canonical correlation analysis.

Another guise is *discriminant analysis*. Again objects are categorized in subgroups, in this case not so much on the basis of conditions created by an experimenter as on the basis of categories of an observed variable (such as ethnic groups, political preferences). Subgroups again can be coded in an indicator matrix, and the problem again becomes the same as in canonical analysis. The direction of the dependence could be in either way. One may, for example, want to find out whether political preference depends on such variables as $y_1 = $ age, $y_2 = $

income. Conversely, one might be interested to see to what extent economic variables like y_1 = income, y_2 = house rent, etc., depend on ethnic identification. Discriminant analysis may also serve the purpose of classification. The typical example is that patients with brain disease can be classified into specific types of disease with certainty only on the basis of autopsy. Suppose that patients with different types of disease were found to have shown different patterns of performance on a number of perceptual or psychomotor tests during an early stage of their illness. This then makes it possible to make a tentative diagnosis during the early stages.

(3) Whereas dependence analysis assumes that variables can be divided into two subsets of variables, other types of MVA focus on interrelations between variables belonging to one and the same set. This sometimes is called analysis of *interdependence*. A typical example is *principal components analysis*. 'Components' are defined here as weighted sums of the observed variables, with the requirement that such weighted sums must be highly correlated with all individual observed variables. Conversely, it will then become possible to express observed variables as weighted sums of components. If this is feasible for a data matrix with many variables and only a few components, we have a clear case of *data reduction*. Let us suppose that one has collected performance scores for a number of children of age ten on a number of mental tests. Suppose one finds a component highly correlated with all tests which can be characterized as 'numerical', and another component highly correlated with all 'verbal' tests. Individual scores on the numerical component can then be identified as a certain weighted sum of the 'numerical tests', and individual scores on the verbal component as a weighted sum of the 'verbal tests'. Conversely, an individual's score on some observed test could be expressed as a weighted sum of this individual's 'numerical score' and 'verbal score'.

A variety of principal components analysis is *principal factor analysis*. The basic diference is that in factor analysis it is assumed that observed variables are subject to random measurement error, with the consequence that a weighted sum of observed variables will also be subject to random error, and therefore can only be an approximation of the 'true' underlying component. Factor analysis has been developed mainly in psychology, since 1900. There is a huge literature on factor analysis, in which very many varieties are discussed (Mulaik, 1972).

(4) Thus far we have discussed *linear* MVA. This means that in interdependence analysis all of the variables are numerical, and that in dependence analysis at least one of the two sets contains numerical variables. Linear MVA prescribes that observations on numerical variables may be transformed only by linear transformation – the usual type of linear transformation is that one takes deviations from the mean instead of raw scores, or that one changes the unit of measurement.

A variable is treated as *nominal* or *categorical* if it just sorts objects into different categories, without concern about how these categories might be ordered, or how differences between categories might be scaled. Examples are political preference, or ethnic identification. Multivariate analysis of such categorical data has been developed along its own lines, more or less independently from linear MVA. Usually, the basic data are in the format of a frequency table – the characteristic example is that rows of such a table sort persons by colour of hair, and columns sort persons by colour of eyes. (Specific solutions for such type of data are described in Goodman, 1978.) However, observations on nominal variables can also be brought within the framework indicated above, in that each nominal variance is coded in the format of an indicator matrix. For example, with two nominal variables, we obtain two indicator matrices, and we are back once again to the canonical analysis situation. Solutions of this kind are proposed by Benzécri (1973), under the name 'correspondence analysis'. With more than two categorical variables, one enters the field of *non-linear* MVA, meaning that categories of a variable can be quantified in any suitable way – the subject is dealt with extensively in Gifi (1982).

(5) An intermediate variety of MVA is *ordinal* MVA, where it is prescribed that categories of variables may be quantified with the restriction that this quantification has a certain prescribed order. The subject is treated in Gifi (1982), where

the mixed case (some variables numerical, other variables nominal, and again other variables ordinal) is also discussed.

(6) The history of MVA shows a bifurcation. Linear MVA has been developed mainly in relation to statistical assumptions; in particular that data were sampled from a multinormal population. Applications of MVA then focus on statistical tests. Kshirsagar (1978) is a typical example of this approach. It implies that very severe restrictions are put upon population parameters, and that sample characteristics must either refute such restrictions, or not. In recent years another approach to MVA came into focus. It is often called the 'data theorist' approach (as contrasted to that of the 'statistician'). Whereas the statistician's approach evaluates observed data on the basis of very specific assumptions about the population from which data are sampled (such assumptions might very well be wrong), the data theorist pays more attention to the 'intrinsic appeal of the data themselves'. The statistician's approach makes generalization possible, at the cost of perhaps unrealistic assumptions about a population, whereas the data theorist is not so much concerned about generalization beyond the sample. Obviously, this controversy is somewhat exaggerated: data theorists should be prepared to consider that sample fluctuations must be taken seriously, whereas statisticians should realize that the multinormal model, although convenient from the point of view of statistical theory, might be far too restrictive from the point of view of how observed data can be generalized. Whereas Kshirsagar (1978) emphasizes the statistician's point of view, Gnanadesikan (1977) or Green and Carroll (1976) emphasize the intrinsic appeal of the data themselves.

John van de Geer
University of Leiden

References
Benzécri, J. P. *et al.* (1973), *Analyse des données* (2 vols), Paris.
Gifi, A. (1982), *Non-Linear Multivariate Analysis*, Leiden.
Gnanadesikan, R. (1977), *Methods for the Statistical Analysis of Multivariate Observations*, New York.

Goodman, L. A. (1978), *Analyzing Qualitative Categorical Data, Loglinear Models, and Latent Structure Analysis*, Reading, Mass.

Green, P. E. and Carroll, J. D. (1976), *Mathematical Tools for Applied Multivariate Analysis*, New York.

Kshirsagar, A. M. (1978), *Multivariate Analysis*, New York.

Mulaik, S. A. (1972), *The Foundation of Factor Analysis*, New York.

See also: *categorical data; measures of central tendency and dispersion; regression; statistical reasoning.*

Networks

One of the perennial problems social scientists face is to relate such abstract concepts as society, institution, and group to the activities and relations of actual people. One approach to this problem is to view the circles of relatives and friends, groups and institutional complexes as social networks that link people at various levels.

The concept of social network was first introduced by Radcliffe-Brown in 1940 and used by Barnes (1954) and Bott (1957) in the mid-1950s. Many anthropologists continued to develop network analysis over the next fifteen years, after which sociologists and political scientists took over from them. The enthusiasm for network analysis was related to the theoretical shift away from structural-functional analysis which by 1960 had dominated social sciences in Britain and the United States for thirty years. The network concept permitted the entry on a systematic basis of interacting people engaged in actions that could alter the institutions in which they participated. This introduced a new dimension into the self-regulating structural-functional edifice of corporate groups, systems and moral order seen as impinging upon people, moulding their character and determining their behaviour. Network analysis provided down-to-earth data.

Social networks have been observed to have a definite structure which influences behaviour and aspects of personality. They are influenced, in their turn, by biological factors, physical environment, residence and climate, but also by ideology.

The patterned characteristics of social networks can be divided into interactional and structural criteria. There are four important interactional criteria: (1) Multiplexity: this is the degree to which relations between persons are single or multiple. (2) The transactional content of a relation: the nature of the goods and services, the degree of emotional involvement, the confidences which are exchanged between people who are linked to one another. (3) The directional flow of the things exchanged: most relations are uneven. Asymmetry in the transactions between two people is an indication of the differences in social status and relative power. (4) The frequency and duration of interaction can also be an important indication of the quality in the content of the relation.

There are also at least four significant structural criteria: (1) *Size*: A person can come into contact with many more people than those to whom he is directly linked. Through his direct contacts, sometimes referred to as his first-order zone, he can come into contact with other persons. These form second-order zones. These friends-of-friends form an important category. (2) *Density*: This is the degree to which members of a person's network are in touch with one another independently of him. Density can be expressed as the extent to which links which could possibly exist among persons do in fact exist. This can be calculated by means of a simple formula: $\frac{100\,NA}{\frac{1}{2}N(N-1)}$ where NA = the total number of actual relations and N = the total number of persons in the network. The density of a network is an indication of the potential communication between members of a network. It is usually assumed, although this must be carefully investigated, that where the density of a network is high, there is considerable social communication and thus increased social pressure for conformity. (3) *Centralilty*: This is an index of the accessibility to one another of members of the network. The more central a person is, the better able he is to bring about communication. (4) *Clustering*: This is the degree to which members of a network form clusters of persons who are more closely linked to one another than they are to the rest of the network. The presence of such clusters, if perceived by a person, influences his behaviour. A person linked to several clusters in his own personal network, each of which has slightly different norms, will have to adjust his behaviour accordingly.

Network analysis complements other research techniques in a number of ways: it focuses systematically on interlinkages and interdependences between units of analysis. This focus embraces micro and macro levels in one analytical framework. It provides a systematic framework for analysing tension and asymmetry in social relations and consequently highlights their inherent dynamics. By concentrating on interrelation, interdependency, and interaction, it yields insights into forms of social organization that emerge from interaction, such as patron-client chains, cliques, factions and other coalitions which, until the network revival, had generally been ignored. It provides a means of relating formal, abstract sociological analysis to everyday experience, for it links interpersonal relations to institutions. Finally, it brings into sociological focus the ill-defined but important category of friends-of-friends.

Network analysis has offered important insights into urban/rural contrasts, male/female relationships, kinship in industrialized societies, the way leaders recruit and manipulate support, and the way in which gossip circulates. It has also been used to combat organized crime and to delineate overlapping positions from which power is exercised through interlocking company directorships.

There are some problems and difficulties associated with this type of analysis: (1) Methodological involution. Network analysis has borrowed heavily from mathematical graph theory. Analytical rigour in this field easily leads to methodological refinements remote from human beings. (2) The danger in regarding network as an object of study in its own right, which is sterile, rather than using the analysis to answer questions. (3) Attributing specific contents to relations between people who are shown to figure in the same network. Network analysis, for example, can plot the linkage between businessmen via overlapping directorships, or between *mafiosi* and politicians. This suggests collusions, but it does not demonstrate it. To do that, the actual exchange content of the relations must be studied. (4) The researcher may be trying to explain too much by network analysis. While it can provide insights into, for example, the movement and location of migrants, it cannot explain the long-term social processes that underlie migration (Boissevain, 1979).

Basically, however, network analysis is very uncomplicated: it asks questions about who is linked to whom, the nature of that linkage, and how the nature of the linkage affects behaviour. These are relatively straightforward questions, the resolution of which is fairly simple. They should form part of the basic research tool kit of every fieldworker.

Jeremy Boissevain
University of Amsterdam

References

Barnes, J. A. (1954), 'Class and committees in a Norwegian island parish', *Human Relations*, 7.

Boissevain, J. (1979), 'Network analysis: a reappraisal', *Current Anthropology*, 20.

Bott, E. (1957), *Family and Social Network*, London, 2nd edn, 1971.

Radcliffe-Brown, A. R. (1940), 'On social structure', *Journal of the Royal Anthropological Institute*, 70.

Further Reading

Barnes, J. A. (1972), *Social Networks*, Reading, Mass.

Boissevain, J. (1974), *Friends of Friends: Networks, Manipulators and Coalitions*, Oxford.

See also: *graph theory*.

Opinion Polls

Opinion polls ascertain public opinion via direct enumeration, as distinguished from reliance upon secondary sources such as content analysis of documents or consultation with influential public figures. The sample survey is the usual technique employed by pollsters, though conceivably a tiny population might be polled in its entirety. Polling traditionally is associated with commercial organizations, rather than with academic research. The importance of the distinction lies more in the style of analysis than in the form of opinion data. The commercial poll-taker's interest rests largely with the face-value meaning of opinion questions, illustrated for example when a newspaper reports the percentage of a population approving of a prominent politician. The academic researcher is more likely to treat opinion poll items as indicators of a more abstract underlying concept, and seek to identify the factors accounting for how people score on the concept.

As the term itself suggests, polling is closely associated with the measurement of political opinion, though the pollster's interests embrace more than politics alone. Polling of opinion in any sphere can be controversial, but it is in the political arena that the issues appear in particularly sharp relief and prominence in the public consciousness. Much debated, both among the public and among professional social scientists, is the *impact* of polling on opinion formation. Polling results, particularly when receiving the wide publicity characteristic of election poll data, may in an ironic inversion become active ingredients in the formation of opinion. Thus, the very polls which are championed as valuable servants of the public – the 'pulse of democracy', as George Gallup (1940) phrased it – may also hold sway as masters of public opinion. If polls determine opinion, there is the irresistible temptation for benefactors of a favourable poll result – a candidate for political office, for example – to load question wordings.

This latter concern brings us to questions of the *accuracy* of polling. Opinion polls tarnished their image through faulty methods of sampling in the 1930s days of sample surveying. Today, much progress has been registered over the technical difficulties of gathering random samples of human populations. Assuming impeccable ethics by pollsters and their customers, the best of sampling procedures, and perfect response rates, however, more fundamental doubts about the accuracy of polls may be entertained. The superficial probes necessary for an enumeration of several hundreds of citizens dispersed over a wide area cannot, it is sometimes argued, capture some funda-mental attitudes. The relentless counting of surface opinion – views hastily offered on sometimes trivial events – ungrounded in either the context of surrounding circumstances or in some basic psychological attitude-set, debases the exercise in the view of some students of mass communications and political sociology.

Justifiably or not, opinion polling has grown into a thriving commercial industry and is part of the institutional landscape of modern industrial societies. At their best, the polls inform, entertain, and, arguably, indeed do lubricate public discourse.

John Goyder
University of Waterloo

Further Reading
Gallup, G. and Rae, S. F. (1949), *The Pulse of Democracy*, New York.
Wheeler, M. (1976), *Lies, Damn Lies, and Statistics: The Manipulation of Public Opinion in America*, New York.
See also: *marketing research; sample surveys.*

Path Analysis

Path analysis is a suite of techniques for estimating and interpreting simultaneous linear equation systems. The model is interpreted by decomposing total effects into direct, indirect, and joint effects. Every model is accompanied by a heuristic diagram.

If y denotes a vector of dependent variables, x a vector in independent variables, and ϵ a vector of disturbance terms, the equation system can be written as $By = \Gamma x + \epsilon$ with B and Γ as coefficient matrices. The variance-covariance matrix for the disturbance terms is ϕ. Path analysis provides estimates of elements of B, Γ, and ϕ which are viewed as parameters of the model. These estimates form the basis for an interpretation of the estimated model which is provided by the analyst.

As there has to be enough information, in terms of the number of variances and covariances in the data, all such equation systems confront the identification problem – a logical problem – forcing the prior setting of some elements in the three matrices being estimated. In the simplest (and majority) of path analyses, B is assumed triangular and ϕ diagonal. For these recursive systems, ordinary least squares (OLS) is the optimal estimation procedure.

Path analysis has been extended to deal with reciprocal effects, feedback loops, and correlation between disturbances. For such models and those with unmeasured variables, and/or multiple indicators of variables, OLS is no longer optimal, and a variety of methods exist for estimating single equations in the system or the entire system. However, with the recognition of system estimation, path analysis has given way to LISREL, a powerful full information maximum likelihood method.

Patrick Doreian
University of Pittsburgh

Further Reading

Duncan, O. D. (1966), 'Path analysis: sociological examples', *American Journal of Sociology*, 72.

Sobel, M. E. (1982), 'Asymptotic confidence intervals for indirect effects in structural equation models', *Social Methodology*.

Popper, Karl Raimund (1902–)

Sir Karl Popper is one of the most creative, wide-ranging and controversial philosophers of the twentieth century. Sir Peter Medawar, Nobel laureate in physiology and medicine, has called Popper 'incomparably the greatest philosopher of science that has ever been'. Yet virtually every one of Popper's many contributions – to logic, probability theory, methodology, evolutionary epistemology, quantum physics, social and political philosophy, and intellectual history – is heatedly disputed by professional philosophers.

Popper was born in Vienna in 1902, studied physics, philosophy and music at the University of Vienna, and left Vienna in January 1937 to become senior lecturer in philosophy at Canterbury University College in Christchurch, New Zealand. He was appointed to the staff of The London School of Economics and Political Science in 1945, and became professor of logic and scientific method there in 1949, and remained there until his retirement in 1969. He was knighted in 1965 and made a Companion of Honour in 1982.

His first and most important work is *Logik der Forschung*

(1934), published in English translation as *The Logic of Scientific Discovery* (1959), which challenged the main tenets of the positivist philosophers of Popper's native Vienna. An ardent advocate of reason and the scientific spirit, Popper nonetheless denied the very existence of scientific induction, argued that probability (in the sense of the probability calculus) could not be used to evaluate universal scientific theories, disputed the importance of the verification (as opposed to falsification) of hypotheses, denied the importance of meaning analysis in most branches of philosophy and in science, and introduced his famous falsifiability criterion of demarcation to distinguish science from ideology and metaphysics.

This early clash with positivism has set the tone and the underlying themes for much of the later controversy over Popper's ideas: at a time when most physicists and philosophers of physics are inductivist, subjectivist, positivist, instrumentalist, Popper remains deductivist, realist, anti-positivist, anti-instrumentalist.

The chief ideas of Popper's philosophy all relate to the basic anti-reductionist theme – first announced explicitly in *The Self and Its Brain* (1977) (written with Sir John Eccles) – that 'something can come from nothing'. Scientific theories introduce new forms into the universe and cannot be reduced to observations, contrary to proponents of induction. The future is not contained in the present or the past. There is indeterminism in physics, and also in history – not only because of physical indeterminism, but also because new scientific ideas affect history and thus the course of the physical universe. There is genuine emergence in biology. Value cannot be reduced to fact; mind cannot be reduced to matter. Descriptive and argumentative levels of language cannot be reduced to expressive and signal levels. Consciousness is the spearhead of evolution, and the products of consciousness are not determined. Nonetheless, the Copenhagen interpretation of quantum mechanics – which is often used to introduce consciousness or the 'observer' into the heart of physics – is rejected by Popper, who maintains that quantum physics is just as objective as classical physics.

Although Popper is first and foremost a physicist, all of his thought is nonetheless permeated by an evolutionary,

Darwinian outlook; and biology has come to dominate his later thinking, particularly his *Objective Knowledge* (1972). His most important contributions to social and political philosophy are *The Open Society and Its Enemies* (1945) and *The Poverty of Historicism* (1957), works both in intellectual history and in the methodology of the social sciences, which dispute the main themes of Marxism and of social planning. The idea of 'piecemeal social engineering' which Popper introduced in these works has had an important influence on practical politicians in the West, particularly in England, Germany, and Italy.

W. W. Bartley, III
The Hoover Institution, Stanford University

Further Reading

Other Works by Popper:
Conjectures and Refutations, 1963.
Unended Quest, 1974.
The Open Universe, 1982.
Quantum Theory and the Schism in Physics, 1982.
Realism and the Aim of Science, 1983.

Works about Popper:
Bartley, W. W. III (1976–82), 'The Philosophy of Karl Popper' (3 parts), *Philosophia*.
Bunge, M. (ed.) (1964), *The Critical Approach to Science and Philosophy*, Chicago.
Schilpp, P. A. (ed.) (1974), *The Philosophy of Karl Popper*, la Salle, Ill.

Population Projections

Population projections are calculations that illustrate the development of populations when certain assumptions are made about the course of future population growth. Projections can be made for the country as a whole, for major geographical or political subdivisions of a country, or for particular classes of a population. The assumptions of the projection may mirror patterns of growth observed in the past, may be based on an extrapolation of past trends, or may be conjectural, speculative or illustrative. The length of the projection period may vary from a few years to many decades, depending on the needs being served, the population in question and the availability of resources.

Several procedures for projecting populations can be distinguished. A total population can be projected forward in time by means of a balancing equation, whereby future population size is estimated by adding to a previously enumerated population changes over the intervening period due to natural increase (births less deaths) and net migration. The method demands a satisfactory initial population count and reliable estimates of the components of population growth, and is warranted only for fairly short projection periods.

A slightly different approach can be taken by projecting an initial population by reference to a rate of annual increase under the assumption of a mathematical model for the form of population growth. The most commonly used model is that of exponential growth. The technique also permits calculations of a population's doubling time, or the rate of growth that must have been operating to produce a particular population size after a certain number of years. Variants of the method incorporate other patterns of growth, such as the logistic, but have the common feature that future population size is estimated without regard to the components of growth.

If a population's age structure is not constant, because of past fluctuations in vital rates or age-selective migration, it is greatly preferable to extrapolate from a known age structure on the basis of age-specific fertility and mortality rates. This is known as the component method of population projection, and is performed in several steps. The first is to calculate the survivors of the initial population on the basis of an assumed or underlying life table, and the second is to calculate the children born and surviving over the projection period. Thus, for example, with a projection period of five years, one would calculate the survivors of people initially aged 0–4 years, 5–9 years, and so on, to give the numbers aged 5–9, 10–14 and so on, in the projected population, and then apply age-specific fertility rates to women in the childbearing years to derive the number of children whose survivors will go to make up the 0–4 age group in the projected population. A final refinement might be to adjust for known or assumed rates of immigration and emigration.

Demographers are perhaps best known for making population projections. Nevertheless, there is a considerable difference of opinion within the profession as to the role of the demographer in this regard, and even as to the function of a projection. According to Brass (1974), 'the forecasting of future populations would seem to many people the main practical justification for the science of demography'. Opposing this view Grebenik (1974) declared that, 'it is perhaps salutary to remind ourselves that there is only one feature that all demographic predictions have had in common, and that is that they have all been falsified by events'. We can go some way towards reconciling these points of view by distinguishing, as does Keyfitz, between a prediction of what will actually happen in the future, and a projection, which is merely the numerical consequence of a series of assumptions. A projection is bound to be correct (barring arithmetic error), while a single forecast is nearly certain to be invalidated by subsequent events. For example, a forecast might be based on current mortality which is subject to change, or on an assumed future level of mortality which proves to have been incorrect.

Whatever limitation or qualifications a demographer places on his projections, he cannot prevent their being used as forecasts. The most he can do is to state his assumptions clearly, or perhaps even prepare a range of projections from a range of extreme assumptions, and leave the user to decide whether any sort of forecast is feasible.

Michael Bracher
Australian National University, Canberra

References

Brass, W. (1974), 'Perspectives in population prediction: illustrated by the statistics of England and Wales' (with discussion), *Journal of the Royal Statistical Society, Series A*, 137(4).

Grebenik, E. (1974), 'Discussion', in W. Brass, *Journal of the Royal Statistical Society, Series A*, 137(4).

Keyfitz, N. (1972), 'On future population', *Journal of the American Statistical Association*, 67.

Further Reading

Dorn, H. F. (1950), 'Pitfalls in population forecasts and projections', *Journal of the American Statistical Association*, 45.

Hajnal, J. (1955), 'The prospects for population forecasts', *Journal of the American Statistical Association*, 50.

Shyrock, H. S., Siegal, J. S. and Associates (1973), *The Methods and Material of Demography*, U.S. Bureau of the Census, Washington DC.

Positivism

Although the explicit postulates of logical positivism are not accepted by most practising social scientists today, there remains an amorphous and implicit self-consciousness, a self-perception, that pervades contemporary social science practice which may be called the 'positivist persuasion'. The major postulates of this persuasion follow.

(1) A radical break exists between empirical observations and non-empirical statements. This seems like a simple and rather commonsensical position, but it is actually a fundamental, specifically intellectual, principle that has enormous ramifications.

(2) Because of this assumed break between general statements and observations, it is widely believed that more general intellectual issues – philosophical or metaphysical – are not fundamentally significant for the practice of an empirically oriented discipline.

(3) Since such an elimination of the non-empirical (purely intellectual) reference is taken to be the distinguishing feature of the *natural* sciences, it is believed that any objective study of society must assume a natural 'scientific' self-consciousness.

(4) Questions which are of a theoretical or general nature can correctly be dealt with only in relation to empirical observations. There are three important corollaries of this fourth point: (a) Regarding the *formulation* of scientific theories, the

positivist persuasion argues that the process of theory formation should be one of construction through generalization, a construction consisting of inductions from observation. (b) Regarding the problem of theoretical *conflict*, the positivist persuasion argues that empirical tests must in every case be the final arbiter between theoretical disputes. It is 'crucial experiments' rather than conceptual dispute that determine the outcome of competition between theories. (c) If the formulation of theories and the conflict between them can be entirely reduced to *empirical* material, there can be no long-term basis for structured kinds of scientific *disagreement*. Social-scientific development is viewed as a basically progressive one, that is, as linear and cumulative, and the segmentation or internal differentiation of a scientific field is viewed as the product of specialization rather than the result of generalized, non-empirical disagreement. It is viewed, in other words, as the result of focusing on different aspects of empirical reality rather than of seeking to explain the same element of empirical reality in different ways.

The ramifications of these beliefs about social science have been enormous: everywhere they have had an impoverishing effect on the social-scientific imagination, in both its empirical and theoretical modes.

By unduly emphasizing the observational and verificational dimensions of empirical practice, the positivist impetus has severely narrowed the range of empirical analysis. The fear of speculation has technicalized social science and driven it toward false precision and trivial correlational studies. This flight from generality has only contributed further to the inevitable atomization of social-scientific knowledge.

This positivist impetus has also led to a surplus of energy devoted to methodological rather than conceptual innovation, for the scientific challenge is increasingly understood to be the achievement of ever more pure forms of observational expression.

Finally, but perhaps most significantly, the positivist persuasion has crippled the practice of theoretical sociology as well. It has sharply reduced the quantity of discussion that directly concerns itself with the generalized elements of social-scientific thought. But it has also unmistakably reduced the quality. This has occurred because under the rubric of the positivist persuasion, it is much more difficult for theoretical analysis to achieve an adequate self-understanding. The positivist persuasion has caused a widespread 'failure of nerve' in theoretical sociology.

What might an alternative position look like? Clearly, even in the American social science of the last few decades, there has been some alternative put forward. What is usually proposed is some kind of humanistic as compared to scientific approach to empirical study: there is humanistic geography, sociology, political science, psychology, and even, most recently, the humanistic narrative approach in contrast to the analytic approach in history. These humanist alternatives have in common their anti-scientific stances, a position which is held to imply the following: a focus on people rather than external forces; an emphasis on emotions and morality rather than instrumental calculation; interpretive rather than quantitative methods; the ideological commitment to a 'moral' society, one which fights the dangers of technology and positivist science. In the European tradition this purportedly vast dichotomy was formalized by Dilthey as the distinction between *Geisteswissenschaft* and *Naturwissenschaft*, between hermeneutics and science. In its most radical form, the hermeneutical position argues that the uniquely subjective topic of the 'human studies' makes generalizations impossible; in more moderate form it argues that even if some generalizations are possible, our effort must aim only at understanding rather than explanation, hence that casual analysis is the monopoly of natural science.

This distinction between social and natural sciences, which is at the heart of such a humanist position, is an invidious one. Such an alternative to the positivist persuasion is too timid, too self-effacing before the power of the 'big sciences'. It also implies a much too rigid connection between epistemology, method, and ideology. Finally, and this of course is the important point, it is plainly wrong.

The humanistic or hermeneutical alternative to positivism suffers from a misunderstanding of natural science. The post-empiricist philosophy, history, and sociology of science in the last twenty years has conclusively demonstrated that the positivist persuasion has been vastly and irrevocably wrong, not just about the usefulness of the natural science guide to social science, but about natural science itself. From the wide range of this discussion there are certain basic points upon which most of the participants in this movement are agreed. These are the fundamental postulates of the 'post-positivist persuasion', and they all point to the rehabilitation of the theoretical.

(1) First, all scientific data are theoretically informed. The fact/theory distinction is not concrete, does not exist in nature, but is analytic. Calling statements 'observational' is a manner of speech. We use some theories to provide us with the 'hard facts', while we allow others the privilege of 'tentatively' explaining them.

(2) Empirical commitments are not based solely on empirical evidence. The principled rejection of evidence is often the very bedrock upon which the continuity of a theoretical science depends.

(3) The elaboration of general scientific theory is normally dogmatic rather than sceptical. Theoretical formulation does not proceed, as Popper would have it, according to the law of the fiercest struggle for survival: it does not adopt a purely sceptical attitude to generalizations, limiting itself only to falsifiable positions. To the contrary, when a general theoretical position is confronted with contradictory empirical evidence which cannot be simply ignored (which is often the first response), it proceeds to develop *ad hoc* hypotheses and residual categories which allow these anomalous phenomena to be 'explained' in a manner that does not surrender a theory's more general formulations.

(4) Fundamental shifts in scientific belief will occur only when empirical challenges are matched by the availability of alternative theoretical commitments. This background of theoretical change may be invisible, since empirical data give the *appearance* of being concrete (as representing external reality) rather than analytic (representing thought as well). But this appearance is not correct. The struggle between general theoretical positions is among the most powerful energizers of

empirical research, and it must be placed at the heart of major changes in the natural sciences.

These insights take us beyond the hermeneutics-versus-science dichotomy. We can see that science itself is a hermeneutical, subject-related activity. Social studies need not, therefore, withdraw itself from the greater ambitions of science. What they must do is to understand the nature of social science in a radically different way, as a science that must be, from the beginning, explicitly concerned with *theoretical* issues. No doubt this much more subjective understanding of the post-positivist position is depressing to those who hope for, and believe in, an objective science; positivists, indeed, might well view such a position as surrender or defeat. I would strongly disagree. As Raymond Aron once wrote in his elegy to the great positivist philosopher Michael Polanyi: 'To recognize the impossibility of demonstrating an axiom system is not a defeat of the mind, but the recall of the mind to itself.'

Jeffrey C. Alexander
University of California, Los Angeles

Further Reading

Alexander, J. C. (1983), *Theoretical Logic in Sociology*, 2 vols, London.

Frisby, D. (ed.) (1976), *The Positivist Dispute in German Sociology*, London.

Halfpenny, P. (1982), *Positivism and Sociology*, London.

See also: *hermeneutics; philosophy of the social sciences; Popper.*

Projective Methods

Projective methods encompass a wide range of approaches to the assessment of individuals and share the following characteristics: (1) stimulus ambiguity-projective techniques consist of materials that can be interpreted, structured, or responded to in a great many different plausible ways; (2) lack of any one correct or true answer – projective stimuli are not designed to represent or resemble any one specific object of experience; and (3) open-ended, complex, and individualized responses – the subject does not usually provide a simple yes-no or true-false answer, but is given the opportunity to organize or structure his response in a personal or individualized way. Projective methods represent an indirect approach to the assessment of a person. Personality characteristics are revealed while the person is ostensibly doing something else, such as telling a story about a picture, or drawing a person. Proponents of projective techniques claim that the person's subjective experience is revealed through these responses; in this manner, the mainsprings of his social behaviour are expressed.

The term projective methods was coined by Lawrence K. Frank, more than thirty years after projective techniques were introduced. Upon surveying the growing number of these techniques and trying to establish what they had in common, Frank concluded that projective methods provide 'a field with relatively little structure and cultural patterning, so that the personality can project upon that plastic field his way of seeing life, his meanings, significances, patterns, and especially his feelings' (Frank, 1939). This is accomplished by means of projection, that is, attributing one's own traits and characteristics to external stimuli. Frank also spelled out several implications of this position: (1) Projection takes place with a minimum of awareness or conscious control. The person transcends the limits of his self-knowledge and reveals more than he is capable of communicating directly. (2) The ambiguous stimuli of projective techniques serve mainly as stepping stones for self-expression. Their specific characteristics are relatively unimportant. (3) The responses to projective techniques are little influenced by the social situation in which they are presented or by the person's current psychological state; they are based on his enduring personality characteristics.

This conceptualization of projective methods is compatible with psychodynamic theories of personality, such as those of Freud and Jung, which emphasize the importance of unconscious impulses and motives. Responses to projective methods lend themselves easily to interpretation in terms of unconscious drives, intrapsychic conflicts, defences against them, and symbolic representation of these forces.

More recent theoretical formulations have attempted to look at projective techniques from other points of view. Bruner

(1948) forged links between responses to projective stimuli and the principles of the 'hypothesis theory' of perception. In Bruner's view, responses to ambiguous stimuli reflect hypotheses, based on past experience and present expectations. Fulkerson's (1965) point of departure was decision making under conditions of uncertainty. Uncertainty in responding to projective methods is of two kinds: stimulus ambiguity, amply emphasized by Frank and other traditional theorists, and situational ambiguity, somewhat glossed over in these formulations. Fulkerson stressed the conscious choices open to the person: to emit or to withhold a response and how to present or communicate it to the examiner, all on the basis of the person's subjective understanding of the context and purpose of projective examination. Epstein integrated responses to projective stimuli with conflict theory. The situation with which the person is confronted in responding to projective materials arouses a conflict of expression versus inhibition of various drive states. This conflict can result in verbal expression of the impulse in question, its suppression, or various compromise reactions, for example, expressing the drive symbolically, partially, or indirectly.

Since 1900, a multitude of projective techniques have been developed. Of these, four varieties have become prominent: inkblot tests, which require the person to impose meaning upon, and to interpret, inkblots or portions thereof; story-telling tests in which the person is asked to provide an imaginative, dramatic account of a picture; graphic techniques, in which the task is to produce a drawing, of a person, or a house, for example, with a minimum of further specifications; and completion techniques, exemplified by sentence completion in which the person is asked to complete a sentence stem, for example, 'Last summer . . .', 'Whenever I get angry . . .'. Projective techniques have preponderantly relied upon the visual modality for the presentation or production of stimuli. Auditory techniques consisting of vague sounds difficult to recognize or structure have been repeatedly proposed, but have not gained wide acceptance. The same is true of several projective techniques that require tactile exploration of stimuli.

Inkblots were introduced by Hermann Rorschach of Switzerland who developed a test consisting of 10 cards. Rorschach devised a multidimensional scoring system based on content (for example, animal, human, plant, object) as well as determinants (for example, form, movement, colour, shading) and location (for example, whole, large, small, or tiny detail). In the ensuing decades, this test was widely used in clinical and research settings; a research literature came into being numbering by now several thousand studies. Not unexpectedly, the results of this work were divergent and complex; some of it supported, and some of it refuted, Rorschach's and other proponents' claims. In 1961, Wayne Holtzman at the University of Texas succeeded in developing a modern and statistically streamlined inkblot test. Consisting of two forms of 45 inkblots each, it allows only one response per card, makes possible determination of test-retest reliability, and exhibits improved objectivity in scoring. Remarkably, it has supplemented, especially as a research tool, but has not replaced, the Rorschach which its proponents continue to prefer because of its allegedly superior clinical sensitivity and ease of administration.

The most prominent exemplar of the story-telling format is the Thematic Apperception Test introduced in 1935 by Henry A. Murray at Harvard University. Twenty cards are administered to the person who is asked not only to describe what he sees, but to extend the story beyond the present into both past and future and to relate the actions, thoughts and feelings of the people depicted. The resulting imaginative production, in Murray's words, reflects a person's 'regnant preoccupations', his characteristic motives, feelings and fantasies. The voluminous literature about the T.A.T. has demonstrated, but not really explained adequately, how its content relates to overt, observable behaviour.

Graphic approaches are best illustrated by the Draw-a-Person and House-Tree-Person techniques. Their rationale rests on the assumption that the person's own characteristics are reflected, or projected, in response to the minimally brief instructions, such as, 'Draw a person, any kind of a person.'

In the completion techniques, more structure is provided and the person's contribution is concentrated upon a 'gap-filling' activity, as in completing an incomplete sentence or story.

Despite its manifest transparency and the ease with which it can be faked, sentence completion, in light of accumulated research, has proved valuable as an auxiliary avenue for assessing personality.

After over eight decades of use, projective techniques remain controversial. In general, they stand in a nonrandom, but highly imperfect, relationship to their nontest referents. They work better in identifying broad and general tendencies of behaviour than in predicting specific acts. Their continued use and study, despite some loss of popularity in the 1970s, is linked to views which emphasize the importance of a person's subjective experience not only as a determinant of his behaviour, but also as a worthy subject of knowledge in its own right.

Juris G. Draguns
Pennsylvania State University

References

Bruner, J. S. (1948), 'Perceptual theory and the Rorschach test', *Journal of Personality*, 17.

Epstein, S. (1966), 'Some theoretical considerations on the nature of ambiguity and the use of stimulus dimensions in projective techniques', *Journal of Consulting Psychology*, 30.

Frank, L. K. (1939), 'Projective methods for the study of personality', *Journal of Psychology*, 8.

Fulkerson, S. C. (1965). 'Some implications of the new cognitive theory for projective tests', *Journal of Consulting Psychology*, 29.

Further Reading

Rabin, A. J. (ed.) (1981), *Assessment with Projective Techniques: A Concise Introduction*, New York.

Semeonoff, B. (1976), *Projective Techniques*, London.

Questionnaires

Questionnaires pose a structured and standardized set of questions, either to one person, to a small population, or (most commonly) to respondents in a sample survey. Structure here refers to questions appearing in a consistent, predetermined sequence and form. The sequence may be deliberately scrambled, or else arranged according to a logical flow of topics or question formats. A questionnaire might, for example, commence with experiences from the subject's childhood, proceeding through time to the present. Questionnaire items follow characteristic forms: open-ended questions, where respondents fill in the blank, using an original choice of words; or the closed-response format, where responses must conform to options supplied by the interlocutor. Choices are frequently presented in the 'agree-disagree' or 'yes-no' form, or in extended multiple choice arrangements such as the Likert Scale, where several adverbs describe a hierarchy of sentiments such as agreement or favourability. Standardizing the phrasing for each question is a key phase in questionnaire design. Seemingly minor alterations in wording can substantially affect responses, a phenomenon which has generated much methodological research.

Questionnaires are distributed through the mail (perhaps the most usual method), or by hand, through arrangements such as the 'drop-off', where a fieldworker leaves the questionnaire for respondents to complete by themselves, with provision either for mailing the complete form back to the research office, or for a return call by the fieldworker to collect the questionnaire. A questionnaire administered in a face-to-face interview, or over the telephone (growing in popularity among researchers), is generally termed a 'schedule'. In deciding upon one of these methods, researchers balance off costs, probable response rate, and the nature of the questions to be posed.

John Goyder
University of Waterloo

Further Reading
Schuman, H. and Presser, S. (1981), *Questions and Answers in Attitude Surveys*, New York.
See also: *interviews and interviewing*.

Quetelet, Adolphe (1796–1874)

Adolphe Quetelet, a Belgian, was an astonishing polymath – poet, geometer, astronomer, meteorologist, demographer, criminologist, sociologist, statistician and more – who exercised a profound influence over individuals and organizations in many branches of science, and whose work raised questions about the role of the statistical approach in the social sciences which can still be fruitfully debated.

Quetelet's method employed an unbiased accumulation of sufficiently large and extensive data sets, their analysis in a style of remarkable neutrality, and a vivid, often inspiring, account of what might be inferred from the analysis. Embedded in a framework of ethical and humanitarian goals and unmarred by any trace of personal rancour, this method proved, in his lifetime, to be novel, irresistible and timely: the intellectual climate was eager to find a scientific basis for the social reforms that were clearly needed to deal with new economic and political forces.

Quetelet used simple cross-tabulation to reveal associations between social ills and factors that he called 'causes' or 'influences'. Where the latter were not beyond the control of man, the possibility of social amelioration was furthered in memorable sentences such as: 'It is Society that prepares the crime and the criminal is only the instrument that carries it out'; and 'There is a budget that is paid with frightful regularity, that of the prisons . . . and the scaffolds: it is that, above all, that we must try to reduce'.

A long-running controversy developed on the question of Free-will versus Determinism, misled by Quetelet's playful phrase 'frightful regularity' and like examples. These merely referred to the regularity of proportions calculated from repeated large samples of the same, stable population – a simple consequence of the laws of probability. For Quetelet, the problem, such as it was, had a straightforward solution: *individual* free-will was quite compatible with *social* determinism.

Fortunately, neither this controversy, nor the one with Comte about who had priority in coining the term *physique sociale* for their quite different theoretical structures, diminished Quetelet's influence on major thinkers. Karl Marx, for example, made use of Quetelet's methodology in his preparation of a statistical case for economic revolution, a conclusion that the liberal ameliorator in Quetelet might have queried! The eminent statistician Karl Pearson was another Quetelet beneficiary, and not just in the realm of ideas. For Florence Nightingale had admired Quetelet and his works with a religious intensity; this, in turn, probably influenced Galton to support Pearson as the first university professor of statistics *per se*, initiating the English, now worldwide, school of statistics.

Quetelet's role in the organization of nineteenth-century science was no less impressive than his influence on individuals. The landmarks were:

1825 – joint founder of the journal *Correspondance mathématique et physique*;
1826 – initiator of the Royal Observatory of Brussels;
1834 – inspirer of the new Statistical Society of London, later the Royal Statistical Society;
1841 – creator of the Belgian 'Commission Centrale de Statistique';
1853 – President of the First International Congress of Statistics.

As early as the 1820s, Quetelet had absorbed the Laplacian optimism that the exactness of mathematics could be usefully applied to the 'moral and political' sciences, and, with the illumination of a prophet, had seen how this could be done. All that remained was the long process of verification, which was fortunately accomplished before a stroke sadly impaired his faculties in 1855.

We are now free to assess whether Quetelet's optimism at the start and his measured satisfaction at the end of this process were justified. In reading his works, of which the earlier versions are the better organized, it should be possible to divorce this assessment from any prejudices induced by the 'arithmomania' and 'quantophrenia' which infected some of Quetelet's disciples, and which now appears in subdued form as an incantatory methodology in all sciences, not excluding the social.

M. Stone
University College London

Further Reading
Lazarsfeld, P. F. (1961), 'Notes on the history of quantification in sociology: trends, sources and problems', *Isis*, 52.
Lottin, J. (1912), *Quetelet, statisticien et sociologue*, Louvain-Paris.
See also: *statistical reasoning*.

Random Sampling

Random sampling is the basic sampling process that underlies all more complex probability samples – stratified samples, cluster sampling, sequential sampling – as well as inferential statistics. It is based on the probability principle that a truly random selection from a population will on average provide a sample that is representative of all characterstics of it. Thus the same resources devoted to an intensive study of a sample usually yields considerably more information than a census.

The size of sample required to estimate characteristics of the population depends on the precision required and the homogeneity of the characteristics in the population, greater precision and heterogeneity requiring larger samples. Population here refers to any arbitrarily but clearly defined group. The sampling frame is an enumeration of the individuals or units of the population.

Samples are taken by using a table of random numbers to select individuals from the sampling frame. Alternatively a lottery process may be used. The only requirement is that all units must have an equal chance of being drawn with each selection. This is 'sampling with replacement'. Since we are usually concerned with large populations and, in that case, estimates of population values from formulas for replacement and non-replacement sampling are virtually identical, we usually do not replace cases once drawn.

David R. Krathwohl
Syracuse University

See also: *sample surveys*.

Regression

(1) In the simplest case there are two variables X and Y for which n pairs of observations (X_iY_i) are obtained (i = 1,

..., n). The problem of *linear regression* is to identify a solution for a and for b, in such a way that the sum of the squared differences between y_i and $(a + bX_i)$ is minimized. This solution can be calculated as follows:

(i) calculate $D = n.\Sigma X_i^2 - (\Sigma X_i)^2$

(ii) $b = \{n.\Sigma X_i Y_i - (\Sigma X_i).(\Sigma Y_i)\}/D$

(iii) $a = \{(\Sigma Y_i).(\Sigma X_i^2) - (\Sigma X_i).(\Sigma X_i Y_i)\}/D$

Table 1

X	Y	X²	Y²	XY
1	4	1	16	4
1	2	1	4	2
2	5	4	25	10
4	2	16	4	8
7	7	49	49	49
Σ: 15	20	71	98	73

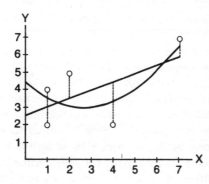

Figure 1: (R68)

A simple example with n = 5 is shown in Table 1. For this example, D = 130, b = 65/130 = .5, a = 325/130 = 2.5.

The figure graphs results. The solution $a + bX_i$ appears in this graph as a straight line (with intercept a and slope b). The solution guarantees that the vertical distances from observations to the line have smallest sum of square – these distances are drawn in the figure as dotted lines.

(2) A generalization is *polynomial regression* where instead of a

straight line a curve is fitted to the observations, corresponding to a polynomial in X_i, defined as $a + b_1X_i + b_2X_i^2 + b_3X_i^3 + \ldots$ In the figure the thin line shows the solution for the best fitting quadratic curve.

(3) Another type of generalization is the case of *multiple regression*, where observations on a variable Y are obtained, together with values for a number of variables X_1, X_2, etc. Assuming that all variables are in deviations from their mean, multiple regression solves for *regression weights* b_j, in such a way that the sum of the squared differences between Y_i and $\{b_1X_{1i} + b_2X_{2i} + b_3X_{3i} + \ldots\}$ has a minimum. The correlation between the last form between brackets and Y_i is called the *multiple correlation*.

(4) From the statistical point of view the linear regression problem assumes that the value of X_i is fixed – not subject to random error – whereas the corresponding value of Y_i is sampled from a population of possible values; Y_i therefore will have a random error component, so that we may write $Y_i = a + \beta X_i + \epsilon_i$. The solution for *a* and *b* calculated on the basis of sampled values then becomes an estimate of the population parameters α and β.

(5) If both X and Y are subject to sampling error, the regression problem changes into a *correlation* problem. In this case there is not only a solution for regression of Y and X (as described in (1) above), but also a solution for regression of X and Y, with roles of X and Y reversed. In a graph, this results into *two* regression lines.

John van de Geer
University of Leiden

See also: *measures of central tendency and dispersion*.

Relativism

The core proposition informing cultural relativism is that the standards which back human cognition are neither absolute nor identical in all societies. Instead, they are cultural in nature and may vary from one society to another. One prescription which relativists draw from this is that what is said and done in any society should be understood in its own terms, according to the standards current in that society. Another is that no basis exists for judgements that the institutions of one culture are superior to those of another. It is especially important to avoid ethnocentrism, that is, the practice of conceptualizing and evaluating what happens in another society against standards drawn from the observer's own society.

One source of cultural relativism is in reports of anthropologists and other travellers that people in various parts of the globe live in successful and productive social orders, although they adhere to standards of truth and morality quite different from those prevailing in the West. In addition, relativism emerged as a reaction to certain tendencies towards intolerance in Western thought. One was the evolutionism which dominated late nineteenth-century anthropology. Closely allied with the idea of progress, evolutionism held that social institutions evolve just as much as natural species do, and that it was possible to arrange the institutions from various human societies on a scale from least to most advanced. It always worked out that Western civilization perched on the top of the evolutionary ladder, while other societies were arrested at one or another of the lower rungs. Charitable Westerners perceived in this circumstance a calling to convert and uplift their less fortunate brethren; tougher-minded imperialists rejoiced in their right, by dint of evolutionary laws such as the survival of the fittest, to exploit their inferiors. In either case, very little in the way of respect, understanding or tolerance was accorded to the institutions of non-Western cultures.

Relativism also grew in reaction to the Romantic idea that people realize their humanity through culture. Stated in those terms, it is a view shared by contemporary anthropology and which is entirely in accord with cultural relativism. Certain variants, however, went on to add the corollary that some peoples are biologically equipped to produce higher levels of culture than others. The most virulent development of such racism, of course, is Nazi ideology.

Anthropology has generated two basic doctrines to combat intolerance and racism: cultural relativism and the psychic unity of mankind. The latter notion – that any normal human infant has the capacity to learn the language and customs and to function as an effective member of any society – is drawn up directly against racism. Cultural relativism counters intolerance at the institutional and cultural level by its denial that cross-cultural evaluations can legitimately be made.

Desirable as its objectives may be, serious philosophical problems have been raised about relativism. If ethical standards may vary among cultures, there is no pan-human morality. Does this commit the relativist to condoning contradictory judgements; to affirm, for example, that to kill a relative of the person who murdered your father is both an exemplary deed (in some societies) and morally wrong (in other societies)? How is the unit within which moral standards operate to be defined? Are minority ethnic groups within a larger society justified in following their separate moral imperatives? Should the same legitimacy be extended to other minorities or subcultures such as terrorist groups or organized crime?

The relativist premise that cognitive standards are culturally variable includes standards of truth and knowledge. Hence, the relativist would have to certify as true a vast collection of propositions, including that witches can kill at a distance; that there is no such thing as witchcraft; that the world is governed by impersonal natural laws; that the world is governed by the will of anthropomorphic beings; and that animals perceive one another as human beings and human beings as animals (Schieffelin, 1976). Is the world big enough, or disorganized enough, to contain a collection of truths such as these? Or is the relativist left with no other course than to conclude that people with different standards of truth inhabit different worlds? Yet precisely what that might mean is far from clear.

One thing it does seem to mean is that relativism is a self-defeating programme. Among the cognitive standards which may vary between cultures are epistemological ones: criteria for what constitutes knowledge and understanding. Presumably the internal understanding counselled by relativism entails that any culture should be understood in terms of its own epistemological standards. It is possible, however, that the epistemological standards in question are different from our own. In that event an internal understanding of the culture would not constitute proper understanding from the perspective of the anthropologist and those who read his reports. The only understanding which would make sense to them would be one that conforms to their own epistemological standards, but they are alien to the culture under examination. Relativism, in other words, appears to rule out the very kind of internal understanding that it is designed to achieve.

Problems such as these are serious enough that few, if any, scholars today defend relativism in its pure form. Some reject it entirely in favour of an absolutist position. But many anthropologists and other thinkers, finding the official disregard for cultural factors in absolutism and the clear ethnocentric tendencies of its practitioners to be at least as problematic as relativism, seek some sort of middle ground. One means of dealing with the moral problem is to attempt to articulate common denominators shared by all or most ethical systems, despite surface differences. Another is to argue that relativism does not commit one to condoning all of the practices which may be encountered. It is one thing to understand that the people who engage in a certain practice consider it to be moral because it conforms to their standards of morality. But the anthropologist's own judgement as to the morality of the practice is an entirely different matter. That depends on the relation of the practice to his own standards, and these may differ from the standards of the culture under study. Understanding, that is to say, does not entail agreeing.

Again, the variability of truth does not necessitate abandoning the notion that all humans inhabit the same world. Truth and knowledge are not contingent solely upon the state of external reality. As C. I. Lewis pointed out long ago (1929), it is inescapable that for any object to be known at all, it must be known in relation to a mind. If the mind were different – if, for example, it operated in terms of other culturally based premises – the description of the object might well be different, and yet it could still be a true description of an independently existing reality.

F. Allan Hanson
University of Kansas

References
Lewis, C. I. (1929), *Mind and the World-Order*, New York.
Schieffelin, E. L. (1976), *The Sorrow of the Lonely and the Burning of the Dancers*, New York.

Further Reading
Hanson, F. A. (1975), *Meaning in Culture*, London.
Hatch, E. (1983), *Culture and Morality*, New York.
Herskovits, M. (1972), *Cultural Relativism*, New York.
Jarvie, I. (1984), *Rationality and Relativism*, London.

Sample Surveys

The modern sample survey evolved from the Victorian social survey movement, which assembled facts about urban poverty. Other sources were the development of the statistical theory of probability, and the early attempts to carry out straw polls before elections. In the twentieth century, Bowley and others used samples in preference to attempts (on-the model of Booth) to survey entire populations. Gradually (and particularly in the United States) the survey was broadened to include questions about attitudes as well as about facts. The surveys increasingly came to focus on the individual rather than on a sometimes ecletic combination of units of analysis, and today the survey normally studies people ('respondents'). Respondents may be questioned about their own lives or asked about the society around them. Information is elicited in answer to questions, often ordered in the formal structure of a questionnaire; but the information may be combined with the fieldworker's own observations. The resulting body of variables (the items of information classified by respondents) is then arranged in a matrix amenable to statistical analysis. Some writers – a minority, however – also use the term surveys for other kinds of data sets, such as aggregated statistics for organizations, social groups, or areal units. In this sense a survey is a non-experimental (*ex post facto*) analysis, to be distinguished from an experimental design.

Sample surveys are intended to provide information about a larger population. The probable accuracy of generalizations from a sample survey to its population can be calculated using the mathematics of significance testing, if certain conditions are met. The most important condition is random sampling; in other words, every member of the population sampled must stand an equal chance of being selected for the sample. For some populations, students enrolled in a school, for instance, random selection poses no obstacle, but for more diverse constituencies true random sampling is virtually impossible. In a national population, which changes constantly as individuals are born, age and die, a sampling frame (a list of all members of the population from which to sample) becomes outdated before it can be used, and it requires a massive effort to compile in the first place. In practice, shortcut approximations to random sampling are generally employed for surveying. Special procedures are then used to estimate the correction factor (termed 'design effect'), to permit the application of significance tests.

But human subjects not only complicate sampling by ageing, changing social characteristics, and shifting residence: they are sometimes not available or not willing to respond to surveys. The study of this 'nonresponse' preoccupies many survey methodologists, and is motivated by both technical and ethical considerations. Technically, only a minor inconvenience – the erosion of the sample case base – results as long as nonresponse occurs at random. Much evidence, however, shows that nonresponse to surveys follows predictable lines. Even if nonresponse derives from a simple availability factor, such as the difficulty of contacting night-shift workers at home during the conventional leisure hours, the resulting uncompleted questionnaires or interview schedules constitute a form of sampling error not accommodated in standard significance testing. An enormous literature on maximizing survey response has accumulated, particularly with reference to mailed questionnaires. Postal surveying counteracts the availability problem, to the extent that people read their mail at a time of their own choosing. Consequently, the elasticity of response due to conditioning becomes evident. Response to mailed questionnaires increases, sometimes dramatically, when follow-up mailings are carried out, or prizes or cash incentives are included with the questionnaire, or even after tests have been conducted to allow for improvements in the covering letter sent out with the questionnaire.

The pursuit of maximum response is sometimes carried to such lengths that ethical issues are raised. If people ignore calls by interviewers or solicitations through the mail by considered choice, should their wishes not be respected? This depends in part on their motives for nonresponse. Many researchers regard principled refusal as very rare, so that in their view the survey fieldworker may be justified in employing persuasive tactics – or as justified as the car salesman or the life-insurance representative. There seems, however, to be increasing sensitivity to the rights of the citizen to privacy and confidentiality, and these rights are now emphasized by the granting agencies which fund much survey research.

Despite problems of these kinds, the sample survey has developed into the dominant method of research in sociology (particularly in the US), and in several of the other social sciences. Not all methodologists applaud this development, and a substantial group prefer such alternatives as participant observation. The survey is especially useful in the collection of comprehensive information about naturally occurring social phenomena. The resultant data may be used either for detailed description or for multivariate analysis, where statistical techniques are used to weigh the influence of various factors on the dependent (to be explained) variable. In either case, the attraction of the survey method lies in its promise to generalize from a sample to a population. A practical difficulty is that survey designs must be determined in advance, and can be altered in mid-study only with great difficulty and expense. Consequently, surveys tend to be employed largely for purposes of confirmation rather than exploration. The logic of the sample survey seems ideally suited to research topics where it is defensible to assume that every sample member's responses are of equal social importance and analytical utility.

One reason that the survey continues to attract social scientists is that it satisfies some key conditions for scientific procedures. The procedures used in a sample survey can be codified, scrutinized, and replicated with a precision denied to less formal methods. The rules for reaching conclusions about the association between variables measured in a survey can be specified in advance (as, for example, when a significance level upon which an hypothesis test will hinge is selected). Social scientists who take the second word of their title literally (too literally, some would argue) tend to be drawn to sample surveys.

John Goyder
University of Waterloo, Ontario

Further Reading
Babbie, E. (1973), *Survey Research Methods*, Belmont, Calif.
Gordon, M. (1973), 'The social survey movement and sociology in the United States', *Social Problems*, 21.
Kish, L. (1965), *Survey Sampling*, New York.
Marsh, C. (1982), *The Survey Method: The Contribution of Surveys to Sociological Explanation*, London.
See also: *marketing research; opinion polls; random sampling.*

Scaling

A social scientist may occasionally be dealing with numerical data representing counts or measurements, but more often with categorical data that can be classified according to some criterion. Categorical data can be bi-categorical (dichotomous) where only two alternatives for a response are available such as yes or no, right or wrong, agree or disagree; they are multi-categorical (polychotomous) where more than two alternatives are available, for example, strong agreement, agreement, neutral, disagreement and strong disagreement. Scaling is defined as assigning numerical values to objects of study – individuals, stimuli, response alternatives or whatever – on the basis of a so-called model of scaling which must be consistent with the data. Such a model may be deterministic or probabilistic.

The basic assumption of all models of scaling, whether deterministic or probabilistic, is that the objects in question can be arranged on one or more underlying or latent continua. In the case of a single latent continuum one speaks of a unidimensional model, and in the case of more continua, of a multidimensional model. The notion of an underlying continuum, whose reality is not directly observable but whose existence is postulated, is essential. Other types of models are conceivable and in fact exist. It may be that the notion of a continuum, though given, is directly observable, such as length measured by means of a yardstick; or it may be that rather than a continuum there exists another underlying mathematical 'object', such as a graph. In such cases one does not speak of scaling in the strict sense of the word.

Models of scaling assume at least one latent continuum, which is referred to as the scale. The objects being studied are represented by points on the scale. Two different possible relations defined upon the points are of importance. In some instances the only thing that counts is the question of whether a point is situated to the right of another point. Such a relation is called an order or dominance relation on points. But what may also be relevant is the nearness or proximity of two points. Such a relation will be called a proximity relation. These relations, whether of dominance or proximity, can also be defined upon the distances between points; however, models with a proximity relation on distances have not yet appeared in the literature. Another distinction is related to the probabilistic nature of the model. One may assume that the position of the point, representing an object on the continuum, is fixed (deterministic models) or random (probabilistic models). Depending on the specific model employed, observations can be classified according to eight kinds of data (see Coombs, 1964).

The capital Q in Table 1 is the first letter of the word

Table 1

The objects come from	Relation between points	Relation between distances
Two sets	single stimulus data: QIIa / QIIb	preferential choice data: QIa / (QIb)
One set	stimulus comparison data: QIIIa / QIIIb	similarities data: QIVa / (QIVb)

quadrant. The distinction between a- and b-data corresponds to the type of relation assumed. In the case of a-data we have an order relation. In the case of b-data it is a proximity relation. For each type of data one has deterministic and probabilistic models. Parentheses refer to data where hardly any models are available. Well-known examples are:

QIa-data:
Coomb's unfolding analysis (Coombs, 1964) which is deterministic and Zinnes and Grigg's probabilistic, multidimensional unfolding analysis (Zinnes and Griggs, 1974);

QIb-data:
no models available yet;

QIIa-data:
Guttman's scalogram analysis (Coombs, 1964), the multidimensional conjunctive-disjunctive and compensatory models (Coombs, 1964) which are deterministic, the logistic model (Lord and Novick, 1968), the normal ogive model (Lord and Novick, 1968) and the Rasch model (Fischer, 1977) which are probabilistic;

QIIb-data:
Coombs's parallelogram analaysis (Coombs, 1964) which is deterministic;

QIIIa-data:
Coombs's triangular analysis (Coombs, 1964) which is deterministic, Thurstone's Model for Comparative Judgment (see Coombs, 1964) and Luce's Choice Model (Coombs, 1964) in many texts referred to as the BTL or Bradley-Terry-Luce model, which both are probabilistic;

QIIIb-data:
the Goodman-Galanter model (Coombs, 1964) which is deterministic and Hefner's model (Coombs, 1964) which is probabilistic;

QIVa-data:
Multidimensional Scaling (Shepard, Romney and Nerlove,

1972), which is deterministic and a multidimensional extension of the model of Zinnes and Griggs mentioned above;

QIVb-data:
Pfanzagl's bisection system (1968), a deterministic model only used in psychophysics.

The models mentioned here as examples hardly represent an exhaustive survey of all the models published in the literature.

The normal ogive model, the logistic model and the Rasch model are usually referred to as ICC models (ICC = item characteristic curve). According to an ICC model the probability of a certain response R is determined by a fixed-scale position for the subject representing his 'ability' and a monotonically increasing function dependent on the item (or stimulus) representing its 'difficulty'. This requires further explanation. According to QIIa data models we have a random scale position $s(i)$ of subject i and a random scale position $s(j)$ of item j both distributed according to some probability distribution. Italicized letters will refer here to random variables. As a result the distribution of the difference $s(j) - s(i)$ also has a certain probability distribution. Usually the assumption is made that $s(j)$ and $s(i)$ are stochastically independent. The probability that subject i reacts to item j with response R is equal to the value of the distribution function of the difference $s(j) - s(i)$ at the point zero. ICC models are a special case of QIIa models under the assumption that the distribution of $s(i)$ only differs in a location parameter a_i:

$$s(i) = a_i + s.$$

Thus the distribution of s does not depend on i but may depend on j. Then the ICC coincides with the distribution function of $s(j) - s$. Let G be defined by

$$G(a_i) = P[s(j) - s(i) < 0] = P[s(j) - s < a_i]$$

then it is obvious that G represents the ICC.

Many numerical scales in psychology are not arrived at by means of a model relating a latent continuum to manifest data, but are generated instead by the subjects directly according to some specified instruction. Well-known examples are the so-called quantitative judgement methods described by Torgerson (1958). However, these methods also make assumptions concerning the numbers produced by the subjects. If these assumptions have testable consequences, then they should be tested in order to validate the procedure.

A. H. G. S. van der Ven
Catholic University of Nijmegen

References

Coombs, C. H. (1964), *A Theory of Data*, New York.

Fischer, G. H. (1977), 'Linear logistic test models: theory and application', in H. Spada and W. F. Kempf (eds), *Structural Models of Thinking and Learning*, Berne.

Lord, F. M. and Novick, M. R. (1968), *Statistical Theories of Mental Test Scores*, Reading, Mass.

Pfanzagl, J. (1968), *Theory of Measurement*, New York.

Shepard, R. N., Romney, A. K. and Nerlove, S. B. (1972), *Multidimensional Scaling, Theory and Applications in the Behavioral Sciences*, New York.

Torgerson, W. S. (1958), *Theory and Methods of Scaling*, New York.

Zinnes, J. L. and Griggs, R. A. (1974), 'Probabilistic, multidimensional unfolding analysis', *Psychometrika*, 39.

See also: *categorical data*.

Set Theory and Algebra

Set theory appears in the foundations of mathematics and is indispensable in many of its branches. As such, it undergirds much of the application of mathematics in the social sciences and, moreover, it provides a natural representation for many relational social phenomena.

A set is a collection of objects, known as elements, which can be specified by a common property or simply listed. In the social sciences, the use of set theory and algebras starts with a specification of the elements in relation to some social phenomenon, data, model or theory. While the use of sets may start with some concrete representation, the concept of a set is an abstraction. Set theory is the mathematical discipline studying the general properties of abstract sets.

Sets (of interest) are taken as subsets of some universal set. Operations can be defined which operate on sets in a universal set to produce other subsets of that universe. The union of two sets A and B, written A ∪ B, is obtained by putting together all elements of A, of B, or of both. The elements common to both A and B form the intersection, written A ∪ B. All elements in a given universe not belonging to A form its complement, A'. Regardless of any empirical content, the operations satisfy general rules, for example, $(A \cup B)' = A' \cup B'$. This is established within set theory and is not subject to empirical verification since it follows from the definition of the operations.

The Cartesian product, A × B, of A and B is the set of all ordered pairs, (a,b), with a from A and b from B. A (binary) relation, λ, between A and B is any subset of A × B. If A and B are the same, we have a relation defined over a set; for example, A is the set of all societies and λ is the relation 'exports to'. These relations may have different properties: reflexive or irreflexive, symmetric or asymmetric, transitive or intransitive, and so on. Different properties define different relation types which have distinctive mathematical properties.

When a set, together with some operations, satisfy a set of specifications (axioms), an algebra results. For example, a Boolean Algebra of sets is a non-empty collection, A, of subsets where (i) if A and B belong to A so do their union and intersection and (ii) if A belongs, then A' does. By taking different sets, operators and axioms, different algebras are formed.

A homomorphism is a correspondence between algebras where some of the algebraic structure in the first is preserved in the second. Homomorphic reduction of one structure to another is a powerful tool, especially for work on structural equivalence.

One area of contemporary social science making heavy use of algebraic representations is social-networks analysis. Graph theory, matrix algebra and algebraic topology see frequent use therein. (*Social Networks* is a new journal whose articles frequently use sets and algebras.)

The art of using algebras involves a judicious matching of

empirical and/or substantive problem with an appropriate algebra, and using the derived theorems of that algebra.

Patrick Doreian
University of Pittsburgh

Further Reading
Kim, K. H. and Roush, F. W. (1980), *Mathematics for Social Scientists*, New York.
Roberts, F. S. (1976), *Discrete Mathematical Models; With Applications to Social, Biological and Environmental Problems*, Englewood Cliffs, N.J.
See also: *graph theory; mathematical models.*

Statistical Reasoning

Statistical reasoning (SR) is a form of reasoning with probabilistic features, applicable to *inference and decision making* in the presence of an uncertainty that cannot be expressed in terms of known and agreed chance probabilities. Thus SR is not relevant to games of pure chance, such as backgammon with well-engineered dice, but is likely to be involved in guessing the voting intentions of an electorate and fixing an advantageous polling date.

Its application is usually mediated by some standard *statistical method* (SM) whose prestige and convenience, especially if computerized, can induce a neglect of the associated SR. Even when explicitly formulated, SR may be *plausible* (*or not*) in appearance and *efficacious* (*or not*) in its ultimate influence. The *evolutionary theory* of SR (Campbell, 1974) postulates that it is a genetically controlled mental activity justified by survival advantage. A related *black-box* view of the efficacy of SR may be useful in deciding between the claims of different SR schools that their respective nostrums are found to 'work in practice'. We will concentrate here, however, on the plausibility of the types of SR usually associated with particular statistical methods, and go on to consider principles that may assist in the continually required discrimination in favour of good SR. Our i[th] example of *method* is denoted by SMi and the jth example of possible *reasoning* for it is denoted by SR_{ij}. Undefined terms will be supposed to have their ordinary interpretations.

SM_1: *The incorporation of an element of objective random sampling in any observations on a population of identifiable items, that ensures for each item a specified, non-negligible probability of being included in the sample.*

$SR1_1$: Without the element of random sampling, it is impossible for the sampler to justify the selection of items without reference to some systematic, comprehensive theory, which may be erroneous or, worse, subject to undeclared or subconscious bias.

$SR1_2$: With the element, it is maintainable by probabilistic argument that the unobserved items should not be systematically different from those observed. This permits tests of hypotheses about the population as a whole.

$SR1_3$: The power of such tests may be enhanced by the device of *restricted randomization* which excludes in advance the selection of samples that would only weakly discriminate among alternative hypotheses.

$SM2$: *Random manipulation of controllable independent variables in the treatment of experimental units, and the analysis of the effect of this manipulation on dependent variables.*

$SR2_1$: If the effect referred to were reliably established, this could be described as *causal*, operating either directly or through the agency of other variables. The use of an isolated random manipulator – uninfluenceable and influential only through controllable independent variables – is necessary in order to rule out the hypothesis of *spurious correlation* between the dependent variables and naturally occurring variation of the independent variables. As a bonus, it also rules out the possibility of the experimenter using 'inside knowledge' to produce such a correlation by unconscious or deliberate choice of the values of the control variables.

SR2$_2$: The extent to which such causal inference is possible in non-experimental investigation depends on the extent to which changes in the independent variables are induced by factors judged to be equivalent to an isolated random manipulator, as in *quasi-experimental studies* (Blalock, 1972).

SM3: *Evaluation of the achieved significance level* P *for the observed value* t *of a test statistic* T *whose (null) distribution is specified by a (null) hypothesis* H$_0$ *i.e.*

$$P = Pr\ (T \geqslant t | H_0).$$

SR3$_1$: When it is small, P provides a *standardized interpretable encoding* of the deviation of t from the values of T that would be expected if H$_0$ were true. Increasing values of t are encoded as decreasing values of P which induce increasing dissatisfaction with H$_0$. A small value of P forces the simple dichotomy: either H$_0$ is true and a rare event has occurred, or H$_0$ does not describe the actual distribution of T.

SR3$_2$: P is *not* the 'probability that H$_0$ is true', which probability is not definable in the set-up of SM3.

SR3$_3$: The 'dissatisfaction' in SR3$_1$ increases *smoothly*: there is no critical value, 0.05 for example, at which P suddenly becomes scientifically important.

SR3$_4$: The *provenance* of T should be taken into account in the calculation of P when, for example, T has been selected as a result of a search for any interesting feature of the data.

SM4: *Calculation, from the data* x, *of a 95 per cent confidence interval* ((x), u(x)) *for a real-valued parameter* θ *in a statistical model defined as a set* {Pr$_\theta$}, *indexed by* θ, *of probability distributions of* X, *the random generic of* x.

SR4$_1$: The particular interval ((x), u(x)) is regarded as relevant to inference about the true value θ because of the *coverage property*.

$$\Pr(\ (X) \leqslant \theta \leqslant u(X)) = 0.95$$

SR4$_2$: The value 0.95 is *not* the 'probability that θ lies in the particular interval $(\ (x), u(x))'$, which probability is not definable in the set-up of SM4.

SR4$_3$: Can the 'relevance' mentioned in SR4$_1$ be reasonably maintained when, as may happen, the calculated interval turns out to be (a) the whole real line, or (b) the empty set, or when it may be logically established that the interval contains θ? Such counter-examples to SR4$_1$ do not arise in the commoner applications of the confidence interval method.

SM5: *Given data* x *for a statistical model indexed by a parameter* θ, *a posterior probability distribution for* θ *is calculated by the Bayesian formula*

$$posterior\ density \propto prior\ density \times \Pr_\theta(x)$$

and used freely for purposes of inference and decision.

SR5$_1$: There are now several nearly equivalent formulations of the Bayesian logic (Fishburn, 1970) whose upshot, roughly, is that any individual, willing to accept a few qualitative axioms about 'probability' and to give expression to them in a rich enough context, will discover that he has a *subjective probability* distribution over everything – or at least over everything related to x. The formula in SM5 is particularly convenient if the first fruits of the introspective process for determining this distribution are (i) the assignment of probability 1 to the assertion that data x was indeed randomly generated by the statistical model and (ii) the probability distribution of θ which is the 'prior density'.

SR5$_2$: If the 'process' in SR5$_1$ were *faithfully* undertaken by a very large number of Bayesians in a range of contexts, then, if the statistical models to which unit probability is assigned were indeed correct, it would be a consequence of the supposed randomness in the models that the data x would, with high probability, show significant departure from its associated model in a specifiable proportion of cases. This would be so, even if the Bayesians were fully aware of the features of their data at the time of their probability assignments.

It may therefore be necessary to defend the rights of Bayesians to use statistical models that would be rejected by other statistical methods.

SR5₃: The difficulty for the Bayesian approach just described may be overcome by the assignment of a probability of $1 - \epsilon$ rather than unity to the statistical model: awkward data can then be accommodated by reserving the prior probability ϵ for any ad hoc models.

SR5₄: A similar loophole may be employed in dealing with the paradox created by data that simultaneously deviates highly significantly from what is expected under a sharp subhypothesis, $\theta = \theta_o$, say, of the model, while *increasing* the odds in favour of θ_o (Lindley, 1957). For example, suppose a 'psychic' correctly predicts 50,500 out of 100,000 tosses of a fair coin and the statistical model is that the number of correct guesses is binomially distributed with probability. For the prior that puts prior possibility $\frac{1}{2}$ at $\theta = \frac{1}{2}$ and $\frac{1}{2}$ uniformly over the interval $(0,1)$, the posterior odds in favour of $\theta = \frac{1}{2}$ are 1.7/1, although the outcome has an achieved significance level of 0.0008.

SR5₅: Bayesians claim that all probabilities are subjective with the possible exception of the quantum theoretic sort. At best, subjective probability distributions may agree to assign unit probability to the same statistical model but, even then, the posterior distributions would differ, reflecting individual priors. Such differences have not succumbed to extensive but largely abortive efforts to promulgate *objective priors* (Zellner, 1980), just as attempts to formalize the apparently reasonable slogan 'Let the data speak for themselves!' have proved nugatory.

SM6: *Given are*
(i) *a statistical model* $\{Pr_\theta\}$,
(ii) *a set* $\{d\}$ *of possible decisions,*

(iii) *a loss function* $L(d,\theta)$, *the loss if decision* d *is taken when* θ *is true*,

(iv) *a set* $\{\delta\}$ *of decision rules, each of which individually specifies the decision to be taken for each possible* x.

Deducible are the 'risk functions of θ, *one for each* δ, *defined by the expectation under* Pr_θ *of the randomly determined loss* $L(\delta(X),\theta)$. *The method, not completely specified, consists in selecting a decision rule from* $\{\delta\}$ *that has a risk function with some optimal character.*

SR6$_1$: The ambiguity of choice of T for the 'achieved significance level' method (SM3), coupled with that method's lack of concern about its performance when H$_o$ does not hold, led Neyman and Pearson to treat testing a hypothesis as what may now be viewed as a special case of SM6. This has, simply, $\{d\}$ = {Accept H$_o$, Reject H$_o$}, L = 0 or 1 according as d is right or wrong and, as a consequence, a risk function equivalent to a statement of the probabilities of error: 'size' and '1 - power'.

SR6$_2$: A difficulty with the risk function approach to inference that is implicit in the Neyman-Pearson treatment of hypothesis testing was pointed out by Cox (1958). It can be illustrated with a simple story. Two pollsters A and B wanted to test the hypothesis that no more than half the electors of a large city, willing to respond to a particular Yes-No question, would do so affirmatively (Cohen, 1969). Pollster A suggested that the poll would require only 100 randomly chosen respondents, whereas B wanted to get 10,000 responses. They agreed (i) to toss a fair coin to decide the sample size, (ii) to employ the 5 per cent hypothesis test, most powerful in detecting a Yes:No ratio of 2:1, with probabilities of error defined before the outcome of the toss is known. They check with a statistician that this test would have an overall power of 99 per cent for the alternative hypothesis that the proportion of yeses was 2/3. In the event, the sample size was 10,000 and the number of yeses was 5678. Both A and B were astonished when advised that this number was too small to reject the hypothesis by the agreed test, even though, had it been obtained in a survey with a non-random choice of the sample size 10,000, it would have had an achieved significance level (SM3) of less than 1 in a million!

The reason for this behaviour is that the Neyman-Pearson lemma, justifying the test, ignores all possibilities other than the null and alternative hypotheses, under both of which any outcome in the region of 5678 yeses has only the remotest possibility of occurring.

SR6$_3$: Another apparent difficulty for risk functions arose in connection with the widespread use of least squares estimates for normal models. Taking risk as mean square error, James and Stein (1961) found that improvements could be made, whatever the true values of the parameters, by means of a special estimator even when this combined the data of quite unrelated problems. This striking phenomenon may be regarded as providing a criticism of least squares estimation viewed as a form of restriction on $\{\delta\}$: a Bayesian approach whose prior insists that the problems are indeed unrelated will not allow any pooling of information – but will also not produce least squares estimates.

The above examples of SR were elicited in response to statements of representative statistical methods and are of a somewhat *ad hoc*, fragmentary character. Are there no general principles that can be brought to bear on any problem of statistical methodology of whatever size and shape? The answer depends very much on the extent to which the 'uncertainty' in the problem has been crystallized in the form of an agreed statistical model $\{Pr_\theta\}$. Given the latter, the ideas of Birnbaum (1969) and Dawid (1977) deserve wider appreciation.

In Dawid's terminology, an 'inference pattern' is any specified function $I(\xi,x)$ of the two arguments: a 'potential experiment' ξ and associated potential data x (the value of variable X). For each ξ in a specified class, a statistical model $\{Pr_\theta\}$ is provided for X, where the parameter θ indexes the supposed common uncertainty in all the potential experiments considered. These are the defining conditions under which a number of principles require that I be the same for data x in ξ and data x' in ξ':

	Principle	*Conditions for $I(\xi,x) = I(\xi',x')$*
(i)	'Distribution'	ξ and ξ' have the same $\{Pr_\theta\}$ and $x = x'$;
(ii)	'Transformation'	ξ' is given by a $1-1$ transformation t of the data in ξ and $x' = t(x)$;
(iii)	'Reduction'	$I(\xi,x)$ is a function of $r(x)$, ξ' is given by reporting the value of r, and $x' = r(x)$;
(iv)	'Ancillarity'	$a(X)$ has a constant distribution (independent of θ), ξ' is the experiment whose statistical model is the set of probability distributions of X given $a(X) = a$, $a(x) = a$ and $x' = x$;
(v)	'Sufficiency'	ξ' reports the value of a sufficient statistic $t(x)$ and $x' = t(x)$;
(vi)	'Likelihood'	the likelihood functions of θ, given x in ξ and given x' in ξ', are proportional

There are implications among such principles so that if one accepts the weaker looking ones, one is then obliged to accept the stronger ones – such as the Likelihood Principle. Very many statistical methods violate the latter.

When there is no agreed statistical model, however, SR cannot receive the (occasionally doubtful) benefit of mathematical support. Perhaps as a consequence, it has not received much attention in the literature, except in the popular texts excellently represented by Huff (1973) or the occasional philosophical article (most philosophical discussions of SR are implicitly model-dependent). At this premodelling level, there is a broad consensus among the statistically-minded as to what constitutes poor SR: it is much more difficult to characterize good SR. The latter is required to avoid the elementary logical pitfalls but has to go well beyond that in constructive directions. A paradoxical snag in statistical thinking about some problems is how to recognize that the data are inadequate to support such thinking: imaginative SR is often needed to specify the kind of data needed to support the embryonic inferences being formulated.

Premodelling SR stands to gain much from the recent advances in 'descriptive statistics' largely associated with the work of Tukey (1977). The techniques of 'exploratory data analysis' and 'computer-intensive methods' (Diaconis and Efron, 1983) extend the range of statistical activity ultimately subject to SR scrutiny but, at the same time, they enhance the risks that SR will be neglected by methodologists fascinated by the complexity of such techniques.

M. Stone
University College London

References

Birnbaum, A. (1969), 'Concepts of statistical evidence', in S. Morgenbesser *et al.* (eds), *Philosophy, Science and Method: Essays in Honor of E. Nagel*, New York.

Blalock, H. M. (1972), *Causal Models in the Social Sciences*, London.

Campbell, D. T. (1974), 'Evolutionary epistemology', in P. A. Schilpp (ed.), *The Philosophy of Karl Popper*, La Salle, Ill.

Cohen, J. (1969), *Statistical Power Analysis for the Behavioral Sciences*, New York.

Cox, D. R. (1958), 'Some problems connected with statistical inference', *Annals of Mathematical Statistics*, 29.

Dawid, A. P. (1977), 'Conformity of inference patterns', in J. R. Barra *et al.* (eds), *Recent Developments in Statistics*, Amsterdam.

Diaconis, P. and Efron, B. (1983), 'Computer-intensive methods in statistics', *Scientific American*, 248.

Fishburn, P. C. (1970), *Utility Theory for Decision Making*, Publications in Operations Research, No. 18, New York.

Huff, D. (1973), *How to Lie with Statistics*, Harmondsworth.

James, W. and Stein, C. (1961), 'Estimation with quadratic loss', *Proceedings of the 4th Berkeley Symposium of Mathematical Statistics and Probability*, 1.

Lindley, D. V. (1957), 'A statistical paradox', *Biometrika*, 44.

Tukey, J. W. (1977), *Exploratory Data Analysis*, Reading, Mass.

Zellner, A. (1980), *Bayesian Analysis in Econometrics and Statistics: Essays in Honor of Harold Jeffreys*, Amsterdam.

See also: *Bayes' theorem; categorical data; measures of central tendency and dispersion; multivariate analysis; regression; stochastic models.*

Stochastic Models

The term stochastic comes from the Greek word *stochos*, meaning a target and suggesting uncertainty. Stochastic models are often used to describe mathematical models with one or more components that depend upon some random variable, that is, a *nondeterministic* or *probabilistic* model.

Deterministic models have a long history in the physical sciences going back at least to Kepler and Newton, and for a long time scientists believed that all natural phenomena should and could be described in terms of deterministic models. The pioneering work of Mendel in genetics, and of various physicists in statistical mechanics, have made the use of probabilistic models commonplace.

In the sense described above, stochastic models include all models used in the statistical analysis of data. In a more restricted sense, stochastic modelling is usually associated with the *theory of stochastic processes*, and is used to describe the probabilistic behaviour of processes evolving or developing in time and/or space. The use of stochastic modelling in the behavioural and social sciences has grown in recent years, and the following applications of general classes of stochastic process models are noteworthy:

> *Random walk*: the movement of stock market prices.
> *Markov chains*: learning models in psychology, social mobility; voting behaviour.
> *Branching processes*: the extinction of family names.
> *Birth and death processes*: the diffusion of news and numbers; demographic models for population growth.
> *Continuous-time Markov processes*: occupational mobility; the study of graded social systems.

An introduction to these and other social science uses of stochastic models can be found in Bartholomew (1982).

Stephen E. Fienberg
Carnegie–Mellon University, Pittsburgh

Reference
Bartholomew, D. J. (1982), *Stochastic Models for Social Processes*,
3rd edn, New York.

Thick Description

Thick description is often used in the sense of the-more-data-
the-better, but this is not quite what Gilbert Ryle (1980), who
coined and defined the phrase, or Clifford Geertz (1973; 1983),
who has made it the cornerstone concept of his interpretive
anthropology, had in mind.

In doing ethnography, 'The aim is to draw large conclusions
from small, but very densely textured facts; to support broad
assertions about the role of culture in the construction of collective life by engaging them exactly with complex specifics'
(Geertz, 1973). Geertz advocates tacking back and forth
between basic questions and exceedingly extended acquaint-
ances with extremely small matters. While not averse to tempor-
arily 'fixing' the flow of social discourse and cultural processes
as 'game', 'drama', 'template', 'web of significance' or 'text',
Geertz hopes to avoid the reifications and reductionism of
method-obsessed, law-seeking social science. Thick description
should be thought of as open-ended, a layering of meaning in
which any bit of behaviour or any statement about human
phenomena can always be further contexted and interpreted by
the next human who comes along.

This insistence on the open and democratic determination of
meaning confronts the worst biodeterminist, rationalist and
élitist social engineering tendencies in social science; but it tends
to gloss over the deepening division of the world into exploiters
and exploited, as well as, for example, the increasing power of
corporate and state-controlled media to define more and more
of everyone's culture.

Geertz's chapter on 'Thick Description' opens his collected
essays, *The Interpretation of Cultures* (1973); and a fine example
closes the collection, 'Deep Play: Notes on a Balinese Cockfight'
(see also Geertz, 1983).

Charles Keil
State University of New York at Buffalo

References

Geertz, C. (1973), *The Interpretation of Cultures*, New York.

Geertz, C. (1983), *Local Knowledge*, New York.

Ryle, G. (1980), *Collected Papers*, Vol. 2, Atlantic Highlands, NJ.

See also: *ethnographic fieldwork*.

Vital Statistics

An individual's entry into or departure from life, or change in civil status, is known as a vital event. In demographic applications the term most commonly encompasses births, marriages and deaths, while including stillbirths as well as live births, and divorces as well as marriages. An exhaustive list of such events would also contain annulments, adoptions, legitimations, recognitions and legal separations, but these latter vital events are less commonly the subject of demographic analysis. Vital statistics are the basic or derived data regarding vital events.

Christenings, marriages and burials were recorded in European parish registers as long ago as the sixteenth century. The first serious study of vital statistics, that of John Graunt in 1662, was based upon burial and christening records and presented the first crude life tables. Civil registration of vital events became compulsory in Scandinavia and some of the American colonies fairly early in the seventeenth century but in England not until 1837, although England was the first country to produce regular publications of vital statistics. In contrast, most developing countries today have either a defective system of vital registration, or none at all.

The information contained in a registration document includes the date and place of the vital event being registered, and the date and place of registration. The sex of the child and names and ages of parents are included on a birth certificate, and the cause of death, and age, marital status and occupation of the deceased on a death certificate. Other information on background characteristics is also obtained, the exact inventory varying with the type of event being registered, and from country to country.

Demographic data are of two types, 'stock' and 'flow', the stocks being population totals at a particular moment and the flows represented by movements into and out of a population over a period of time. Information on stocks is obtained from periodic population censuses or population registers, and on flows from a system of registration of vital events. The most obvious examples of flows are births and deaths, although marriage is also a flow as it represents movement from the unmarried to the married state. The most basic demographic measures incorporate both types of information, with a flow in the numerator and a stock in the denominator. Thus, for example, the crude birth rate, the simplest fertility measure, is calculated as the ratio of births which occurred during a particular year, as obtained from registration data, to the estimated mid-year population. Similarly, the total number of deaths in a particular year is related to the mid-year population in order to estimate the crude death rate.

Such measures can be made more informative by taking into account additional attributes such as age or, depending on the background information collected on the registration forms and its comparability with census information, other characteristics as well. Some examples are life tables for different occupational groups or regional age-specific fertility rates.

Most developing countries, as already noted, lack a comprehensive system of vital registration. In an attempt to compensate for this deficiency a number of techniques have been developed over the last twenty years by which vital rates can be estimated from fairly simple questions appended to a census schedule. Vital rates are also estimated, with varying degrees of success, from specially designed sample surveys.

Gigi Santow
Australian National University, Canberra

References
Shryock, H. S., Siegel, J. S. and Associates (1973), *The Methods and Materials of Demography*, Washington DC.
Spiegelman, M. (1968), *Introduction to Demography*, Cambridge, Mass.

Further Reading

Brass, W. and Coale, A. J. (1968), 'Methods of analysis and estimation', in W. Brass *et al.* (eds), *The Demography of Tropical Africa*, Princeton.

Graunt, J. (1939), *Natural and Political Observations Made upon the Bills of Mortality*, ed. W. F. Willcox, Baltimore.

Wrigley, E. A. and Schofield, R. S. (1983), 'English population history from family reconstitution: summary results 1600–1799', *Population Studies*, 37.